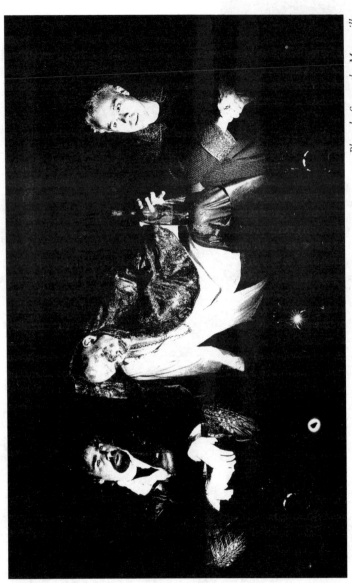

Photo by Samantha Moranville

A scene from the Red Bull Theater production of *The Revenger's Tragedy.* Left to right: Haynes Thigpen as Hippolito, Christopher Oden as the Duke, Matthew Rauch as Vindice.

THE REVENGER'S TRAGEDY

A NEW VERSION BY JESSE BERGER

Freely adapted from the original text by
THOMAS MIDDLETON, CYRIL TOURNEUR
or ANONYMOUS

Incorporating material from the writings of
FRANCIS BACON, JOHN DONNE, THOMAS KYD,
JOHN MARSTON, WILLIAM SHAKESPEARE
and JOHN WEBSTER

★

DRAMATISTS
PLAY SERVICE
INC.

THE REVENGER'S TRAGEDY was produced by Red Bull Theater (Jesse Berger, Artistic Director; Jessica Niebanck, Producing Director) in New York City, opening on November 27, 2005. It was directed by Jesse Berger; the set design was by Evan O'Brient; the lighting design was by Peter West; the costume design was by Clint E. B. Ramos; the mask design was by Emily DeCola; the hair and makeup design were by Erin Kennedy Lunsford; the original music was by Daniel Levy; the property design was by Mary Vorrasi; the choreography was by Tracy Bersley; the fight direction was by J. David Brimmer; and the stage manager was Renee Blinkwolt. The cast was as follows:

VINDICE	Matthew Rauch
HIPPOLITO	Haynes Thigpen
CASTIZA	Naomi Peters
GRATIANA	Petronia Paley
DUKE OF VENICE	Christopher Oden
DUCHESS OF VENICE	Claire Lautier
LUSSURIOSO	Marc Vietor*
SPURIO	Jason C. Brown
AMBITIOSO	Daniel Cameron Talbott
SUPERVACUO	Ryan Farley
FLAMINIO	Russ Salmon
ANTONIO	Paul Niebanck
LUCRETIA	Saudia Davis
PIETRO	Ty Jones
NENCIO	Daryl Lathon
SORDIDO	Aaron Clayton
ANTONIO'S LORD	Yaegel Welch*
SPURIO'S SERVANT	Russ Salmon
FIRST OFFICER	Denis Butkus
SECOND OFFICER	William Peden

* During the New York run, the roles of Lussurioso and Antonio's Lord were also played by Michael Urie and Amefika El-Amin, respectively.

An earlier version of this script was produced by Washington Shakespeare Company (Christopher Henley, Artistic Director; John Emmert, Managing Director) opening on February 1, 2000.

The script was further developed at a reading produced by New York Theater Workshop (James C. Nicola, Artistic Director; Lynn Moffat, Managing Director; Jack Doulin, Casting Director; Linda Chapman, Associate Artistic Director) on March 11, 2002.

ACKNOWLEDGMENTS

Wonderfully talented actors and designers were involved in two productions of this play which I directed. I am especially grateful to my closest collaborators on both productions. I learned an amazing amount from them all, and their contributions are everywhere to be found in this text. As many of them are thanked here as possible, with apologies to any who have been omitted due to space restraints or faulty memory: Aaron Leichter, Aaron Mastin, Allan Buchmann, Ashley Strand, Barbara Hogenson, Blair Singer, Bradley McCormick, Brian Keating, Carlos Bustamante, Caroline Kellogg, Catherine Weidner, Chris McKinney, Christopher Henley, Clark Middleton, Coleman Domingo, Corey Pierno, Daniel Fish, Danielle Streisand, David Chandler, David Grimm, David Levine, Davis Hall, Diego Daniel Pardo, Dylan McCullough, Eleanor Holdridge, Ellen Young, Garin Marschall, George F. Grant, George William Mayer Jr., Gerry Bamman, Gordana Svilar, Graham Hurt, Grant Goodman, Greta C. Dowling, Gregg Bellon, Howard L. Blau, Howard Overshown, Ian LeValley, Ian Strasfogel, Ira Schorr, Jack Doulin, Jack Wetherall, Jack Willis, Jason Loewith, Jeff Biehl, Jennifer Ikeda, Jennifer Phillips, Jenny Cockerham, Jerry Richardson, Jessie Duncanson, Jim Festante, Joan and Steve Young, John Emmert, John Krasinski, Joshua Berger, Jonathan Bailey, Jonathon Church, Jon Dean, Julio Perez, Karma Camp, Katherine Hood, Kate Skinner, Kevin Blomstrom, Kimberly Dilts, Laura Hicks, Lea Umberger, Margaret Currier, Maria Thayer, Marianne Meadows, Mark Gladue, Melinda Basaca, Michael Jerome Johnson, Michael Kahn, Michael Stuhlbarg, Michelle Weiss, Michael Yahn, Molly Tack, New York Theater Workshop, Patrick Darragh, Patrick Sweetman, Peter Haring Judd, Priscilla Mooradian, Randy White, Raul Klein-Aktanov, Ron and Carol Berger, Rosemary Strub, Sandra Garner, Saudia Davis, Scott Barrow, Sean Dugan, Sean Thorne, Seth Reiser, Standing Bear, Stephanie Laffin, Stephanie Wallis, Stephen Shetler, Steve Wilhite, Steven Scott Mazzola, Stuart Howard, Sun King Davis, The Culture Project, Thomas Jay Ryan, Tim Carroll, Tim Getman, Tracy McMullan, Tricia Craig, Vanessa Watters, Waleed F. Zuaiter, and the Washington Shakespeare Company.

ABOUT THE PLAY

So far as revenge is concerned, our society, like that of Jacobean London, is two-faced; while the individual urge to retaliate is natural, our social concern is to keep this instinct in check.

—R.A. Foakes

Corrupt government, hypocrisy, abuse of power, adultery, murder, the death penalty, acts of vengeance, violence and vigilantism. Jacobean tragedy, or the headlines of *The New York Times*? Written during a time of political and social upheaval, *The Revenger's Tragedy* is strikingly of our time as well as its own.

This Jacobean firebrand of a play borrows liberally from the revenge tragedies that preceded it (*The Spanish Tragedy*, *Hamlet*, *King Lear*, *Titus Andronicus*, and *The Malcontent*, among others), baldly using plot devices and characters from other plays, riffing on them, and spinning them together into its own stew of mayhem. The play also steals the old style of medieval morality plays and tosses it into the mix: As in *Everyman*, the characters are named for their chief characteristic, but where in *Everyman* the names are starkly moral ("Good Deeds," "Knowledge," etc.) in *Revenger's* they embody the outrageous behavior of this depraved and imaginary Italian court of Venice ("Lust," "Ambitious," etc.) The play spins these two old forms together into a new kind of tragedy written in a comic rhythm. The scholar R.A. Foakes called it a "tragic burlesque," and the play does seem to be roasting the art of tragic writing for the theater even as it goes about being its own super-ultra revenge tragedy.

Vindice, the "revenger" of the play, is an anti-Hamlet. Where Hamlet deliberates, Vindice acts, often role-playing like mad to achieve his ends. All the characters in *The Revenger's Tragedy* are hyper-aware — they know they are in a play, they know the role they play, and they play it with abandonment until they meet their pre-determined ends in the requisite blood-bathing finale.

Every passion, in excess thereof, is like a short madness, and if it continue vehement and obstinate, commonly ends in insanity.

—Francis Bacon

ABOUT THE AUTHOR(S?)

The Revenger's Tragedy was first performed around 1607, just a few years after *Hamlet*. Although the notion of authorship was not nearly so precious to the playwrights of the Jacobean era as it is to us today, whoever wrote this play may have had some special reason to remain anonymous, perhaps because the play contains such a gleeful advocacy of government overthrow. In 1656, Edward Archer ascribed the play to Cyril Tourneur upon the evidence of the initials "C.T." inscribed upon an original printed text, and the similarity of the title to a play known to be by Tourneur, *The Atheist's Tragedy*. As *The Revenger's Tragedy* began to be performed again in the twentieth century, scholars put forth a convincing argument based on internal linguistic evidence that Thomas Middleton was the author. Middleton wrote over thirty plays and masques, many of them for the Boys of St. Paul's as well as the indoor Blackfriar's Theater. He wrote *Women Beware Women, The Changeling* in collaboration with William Rowley, and he is thought to have contributed scenes to Shakespeare's *Timon of Athens* and *Macbeth*. While it seems more plausible that Middleton wrote the play than Tourneur, any close study or hearing of *The Atheist's Tragedy* will reveal that Tourneur continues to be just as likely a contender. Indeed, one could make a case that almost any of the leading Jacobean authors had a hand in it: John Webster *(The Duchess of Malfi)* and John Marston *(The Malcontent)* seem particularly likely. It is also just as possible that the play is the result of two or more writers working together, a common practice of the time.

In that Jacobean spirit of collaboration, the play you have in your hands interpolates into the original text writings of Francis Bacon, Jesse Berger, John Donne, Thomas Kyd, John Marston, Thomas Middleton, William Shakespeare, Cyril Tourneur, and John Webster.

DIRECTOR'S NOTES

Every director must find his or her own approach to a play, and I encourage future directors to mine their own creativity in bringing this rewarding text to life. I have always found other playwright's and director's notes to contain invaluable advice, and so I have put these thoughts together in the hopes they will be helpful. Use them if they are.

On the other hand, I often find if someone plants an idea about a production in my head too early in the creative process, that it can take months to escape from that idea, whether it was right or wrong for the production I was making. I recommend not reading these notes until you have a clear idea where you want to go with the play. Then my comments can help answer questions for you without stultifying your imagination.

I directed two productions of this play and worked on the text for over five years. Here are some observations from my experiences with it.

STYLE

The play works best when it is dancing on a razor's edge between tragedy and comedy. It is neither *Hamlet* nor *The Rocky Horror Picture Show*. Think of it as the scariest, most truthful, most fun roller coaster you have been on. It works as the best kind of thriller: one that provokes, horrifies, entertains, amuses, and shocks. It should contain a non-stop series of surprises, and play at a relentlessly fierce, fast clip. Nothing is precious.

The play is an indulgence — you must indulge just as far as it will go, but no further — finding those limits is something you will have to discover with your actors and audience. Keep your eye on the ball of the story. You and Vindice must take the audience on the ride, acting as their guide and confidante at every point. They should feel like co-conspirators.

BACK STORY

The Duke and Duchess came to rule in a joint coup ten years ago. Their marriage was part of a power partnership that helped propel them into the palace together.

The old court was Elizabethan and idyllic. The new court is Jacobean and immoral.

Vindice's father was demoted with other folks from the old court like Antonio. Vindice's father returned home, and silently drank himself to death. Since that time, Hippolito slowly worked his way back into court from the lowliest place until we meet him finally working for the Duke's son, Lussurioso. Getting Vindice in to work for Lussurioso will put them both within striking distance of the Duke. This is a plot that Vindice and Hippolito set in motion after Gloriana and their father's death. It is nine years in the making.

Hippolito has made connections with Pietro, Antonio's aide and confidante, and the leader of the only surviving major disaffected faction still at court.

Antonio has lived on the fringes of the court as a shadow government and city conscience. The Duke can't politically afford to have them wiped out completely, so he appeases Antonio, but only in word, never in action. Antonio has a significant discontented following that Pietro and his Lord represent; he is finally planted on the throne by them, his own hands kept remarkably clean from the coup itself.

TIME LINE

The play happens very swiftly, both in the play's time scheme and in real time.

It should play no longer than two hours, without rushing. In New York, the running time was two hours ten minutes, including a fifteen-minute intermission. The ending of one scene often over-lapped with the beginning of the next.

No more than five days pass from the first scene to the last. The rape prologue happens a few days earlier, at most. From the time Vindice and Hippolito kill the Duke until his body is discovered, no more than one day passes. While the Duke is being killed, Lussurioso is being released from prison. Lussurioso passes Ambitioso and Supervacuo on the street back from prison at dawn. Hippolito returns to Lussurioso in Act Two, Scene 2, just hours after burying the Duke's body in the bowels of the palace. None of them have slept when they meet each other in Act Two, Scene 5 (the "malcontent" scene). Lussurioso's coronation happens within hours of his ascension.

AUDIENCE

The play is intensely personal and publicly spectacular. The juxtaposition of Vindice's very private relationship with us and the very public spectacles of what happens at court should be sharply juxtaposed. It is inherently theatrical, and thrives on a direct relationship between the audience and actors. The audience is a character. If you play it right, they will gasp and giggle in equal measure. Even if you are producing this in a large theater, creating a sense of intimacy with the audience is key. Seduce them.

CHARACTERS

All the characters must be played with an operatic intensity. They are driven by their primary characteristic, but they are full-blooded, passionate, outrageously demented people. Despite appearances, this play is an ensemble piece, and works best when everyone is working in tandem like some deranged orchestra, with Vindice as a kind of outrageous guest conductor. In casting, pretty much everyone needs to be able to dance, fight, and be physically distinctive. It can help the audience a lot if you can cast certain families with similar physical traits. For instance, in New York, my Duchess, Ambitioso, Supervacuo, and Flaminio were all blonde-haired (or if not, dyed or wigged so). You might cast Vindice and his family as all one race aside from the rest of the cast. It's not necessary as long as your staging and story-telling is clear, but in any case, the more diverse, the better. It should be a delectably indulgent smorgasbord.

Some thoughts follow for each character.

VINDICE. It is critical that Vindice remain a positive driving force in the play: He knows his role and he revels in it; that's not to say he is over-confident; he is not perfect, and often must improvise wildly. We enjoy watching him set his plot in motion, get caught in traps, get out of them, and ultimately win. He and his brother Hippolito are in it together from beginning to end, and they are almost always having a great time as they risk their lives to skewer the corruption around them.

Vindice's soliloquies have nothing reflective in them. He is the opposite number to Hamlet. His nine-year delay has been all about waiting for the right moment to strike, never a question of whether or not to act and no doubt about his justification for vengeance. Certainly there is a great deal of darkness in Vindice, and his wounds are deep, but there is not time to indulge in watching that sparrow fall — he must act.

There must be a bit of a showman about anyone you cast in this role. In New York, Matthew Rauch struck a perfect balance of deeply-felt fury and playfulness in his role as both our anti-hero and tour guide through the horrors of the court. His growing realization at the depths of depravity at court is part of the journey of the character, and Matthew registered this pitch perfectly. The "thrill-kill" that ends Act One is a turning point for both Vindice and Hippolito — from that point on, they are addicted and the clock is ticking furiously for any further coup to occur — and now Vindice needs to drain the veins from Lussurioso's lust, too! But the tone changes and they become somewhat drunk on the blood-rush of blood-lust, with attendant heightened tensions. At key points along the way, Vindice hits moments of reflection which can only be lightly tapped and then moved on from (e.g., "I think man's happiest when he forgets himself"), but they are important for the character's development towards his ultimate self-sacrifice, and for the audience's journey with him.

Inevitably, the question will arise: Why does he confess? There are two answers: 1) When he tells Antonio that he and Hippolito killed the Duke, he expects to be rewarded — it has not occurred to him that Antonio would condemn him for this — he has purged the Dukedom from corruption, and planted Antonio on the throne! 2) Once Antonio has condemned him, he recognizes his fate, and accepts it with a surprising joy. He has accomplished all he set out to do, and he relishes telling everyone what he did. He has fulfilled his role as the Revenger, and he takes a final bow on his exit. There is no regret in that final speech. The "tragedy" of the revenger is that he must die to achieve his ends. It's a real tour-de-force part — enjoy!

HIPPOLITO. In the New York production, Haynes Thigpen found the greatest balance of humor and intensity in Hippolito, and both he and Mark Gladue (my excellent Hippolito in DC) made clear how vital the role is. Haynes also came up with the notion that the name Hippolito relates to horses in Greek mythology (via Hippolytus) and therefore the character is perhaps obliquely named after the Trojan Horse. This may be a stretch, but it's useful. He is the conduit by which Vindice is able to exact his revenge, and in many ways he is the glue that holds the play together. Don't underestimate the importance of Hippolito because he has less to say than Vindice — his reactions and presence are constantly vital. Sometimes they are like two young boys playing a game, sometimes like a twisted Jacobean Abbott and Costello/Vladimir and Estragon. When Vindice confesses, Hippolito is shocked, but he comes around quickly to a pride that allows him to die without hating his brother.

CASTIZA. She is chaste, strong, and sincere. Just a tad older than Juliet. She is severely shaken by her mother's willingness to prostitute her. Seeing the way of the world, she makes the only strong choice a woman can in this society: to fend for herself. It is frightening for her, but when her mother tries to recant, it only strengthens her resolve. With Lussurioso gone, she finds her way to Antonio.

GRATIANA. She is religious and graceful and it's sincere, but she is in a desperate financial situation. When Piato presents her with enough money to raise the family out of poverty forever, she can't help but jump at it. She is genuinely ashamed of her actions later on, and she must save her soul as best she can. When Castiza leaves her, it is horribly upsetting for her, but she knows Castiza is right on the same level which tempted her before — there is only one way for women to rise in this misogynistic world — Castiza will raise them out of poverty. It is a tricky part that requires tragic stature but walks a thin line just on the edge of comedy. It's not a tragedy: Castiza will send gold, and her sons have forgiven her. "What shall I eat?" is sincere, and funny.

DUKE. Dangerous, outrageous, indulgent, capricious. Bob Hoskins in *The Cook, The Thief, His Wife, and Her Lover* is not a bad model. Or a sort of caricature of Boris Yeltsin/Slobodan Milosevic. He needs to be in good enough shape and strong enough to really do the stage violence at the end of Act One, and also to present a real threat to everyone at court. He must exude extravagant power and danger. The Duke and Antonio should certainly be the oldest people at court, but they are by no means aged or decrepit.

DUCHESS. Lady Macbeth and Tamora, with an insatiable sex drive. She is done with this old Duke sexually; she wants more power for herself — she wants to be Duchess *alone,* with the bastard (or others) as a lover. And then she wants her children on the throne.

LUSSURIOSO. The true nemesis of the play. The Duke represents Vindice's target; Lussurioso becomes his biggest threat and largest obstacle. An equal measure of menace and perversion. In New York, two actors played the role with very different and equally effective results: Marc Vietor was a sensual, somewhat demonically perverted, capriciously dangerous creature of the court; Michael Urie brought a callow youth's sensibility to the role: a spoiled young prince who can have and do anything he wants, a sort of perverted Prince Hal. The role can absorb many different kinds of eccentricity and behavior — what is vital is that he always present a real threat to Vindice and Hippolito. He should not be just a fop. His sex drive is insatiable. He has his every whim catered to, so he's always on the look-out for more interesting ways to get off. Castiza represents that, and Piato is titillating to him, too. He is pan-sexual. After his night in prison, he is furious — he must learn to behave politically, and he tries to be a Machiavel; he proves himself to be both more subtle and more foolish than his father. Once crowned, he is just about to come into his own as a dawning Caligula.

SPURIO. Edmund in *Lear,* although not as clever. Despite his protestations, he starts to like screwing the Duchess, and that distracts him from the job at hand.

AMBITIOSO and SUPERVACUO. Have fun. They really are over the top. Yes, Chiron and Demetrius from *Titus.* One of them is smarter than the other. They must be both deliriously dangerous and frighteningly funny.

FLAMINIO. Nasty, nasty, nasty. Devil-may-care, his momma's the Duchess, so what's to stop him from partying and screwing everything that moves, like his step-dad?

13

ANTONIO. Antonio is all positive. He is a true believer with no malice. Our heart should break for him over Lucretia. He contains a darkness that he cannot control, like Angelo in *Measure for Measure*. His draconian vision is a utopia to him, and there should be no need for him to emphasize the future terror that his new world order implies. He is an imagined conflation of Robespierre, Angelo, Kenneth Starr, and John Ashcroft. In the New York production, Paul Niebanck — a genuinely sweet soul — played him with such sincerity that audiences were seduced by him and genuinely shocked to discover his dark side. We must think he is the good guy, just as Pietro, Vindice, and Hippolito do. He represents the exact opposite side of the coin to the Duke.

LUCRETIA. She's really young, really pure, and she really gets destroyed. She should be stunningly beautiful. Listen to Britten and read Shakespeare's poem.

PIETRO. A true believer in the theories of justice, honor, integrity, and godly future that Antonio has proselytized. He is Antonio's highest apostle, albeit an impatient one like Judas to Jesus — he has waited nine years, too, and the time has come to act. He does not know Antonio has darkness, and sees him as a savior of the people. He is a kind of Alan Keyes, Grover Norquist, or perhaps a young Dick Cheney.

ANTONIO'S LORD. A good, solid, younger version of Pietro. Totally well-intentioned. The fact that he and Pietro participate in the murderous coup and hide this from Antonio does not strike either of them as hypocritical. It was the only way to plant Antonio on the throne, and if their hands had to become sullied to do it, at least Antonio's did not.

NENCIO and SORDIDO. Sycophants. They have thrown their lot in with Lussurioso, and will do anything to stay in his favor and to help plant him on the throne. They have no loyalty to anyone else. They are not servants — they are young lords of the court who have become favorites of the Duke's son, like those to Richard II. There is some homoerotic byplay between them because of who Lussurioso is, but the relationship is based on their sense of entitlement that when Lussurioso becomes Duke, they will be rewarded for their loyalty.

SPURIO'S SERVANT. He's a bit of a bad boy, but he meant well.

FIRST OFFICER. He's not dumb, but he is credulous. A small-town boy trying to make good in the big bad city. Cast someone with good comic timing as a straight man.

SECOND OFFICER. Cast someone strong, tall, in good shape. A good bet for your fight captain.

DESIGN

Set. An open space where swift changes can be made theatrically and dramatically. Don't get bogged down in representational scenery. The play lives very comfortably in a setting which has a lively mixture of Jacobean and contemporary styles, but other imaginary worlds no doubt will serve it just as well. In both my productions, de Chirico was an inspiration, and Venetian archways seem to be *de rigueur*. There should be a sense that people can enter and exit from anywhere. You will probably want at least one trap door. Leave room for surprises. I think the play cries out for an acute sense of being "a stage on stage," a world of proscenium arches, grand red drapes and curtains. In New York, we used a series of red curtains that operated a variety of ways for different locations. Antonio had white curtains, and the red grand drape that had been the only front curtain we knew was supplanted at the end of the play by a white curtain when Antonio took over. Take it or leave it, but if you're looking for an idea, it certainly can work. I always pictured the set within a tunnel: a decadent Venetian palace/opera house sinking beneath the canals into the sewers of Venice — gold leaf in the gutter. Black, gold and red, white for Antonio. Fellini, Versace, Gaultier, de Chirico, El Greco, Peter Greenaway, Verdi ... In New York, we had a beautiful gilt-framed large mirror that dominated the back wall of the set. Peter West lit it brilliantly so that it did not glare in the audience's eyes, and the mirror was just bent enough so as to create a slight fun-house effect. At the final masque of Revenger's, the two groups of terrorist-dancers appeared behind it, and we revealed it to be a two-way see-through mirror. They then dropped out of sight through a trap door, and surprised the group at the table. This worked terrifically. You don't need to use it if you come up with something that fits your theater better. What is vital is that both masques be spectacular.

Costumes. They should be a parade of extravagance and invention. This is a world where clothes can really make the character. In New York, Clint Ramos succeeded in creating an expressionistic tableaux of indulgent Jacobean creatures suffused with contemporary styles. In both my productions, Jean-Paul Gaultier was an inspiration. Embrace the blood — it's necessary to the effectiveness of the play. Find creative ways to get the clothes bloody without having a huge laundry bill.

Lighting. Shafts and shadows. Aggressive use of footlights. Peter West made wonders with about twenty lights in New York. Lots of red and white.

Music/Sound. Music is a vital component and can really help propel the story. In both my productions, I found a mixture of opera and modern classical music to be a great aural backup for the play. Including a mixture of modern rhythms will greatly enhance the contemporary feel of the play, which is desirable. Daniel Levy created an entire score for the play in New York, underscoring the ends of every scene and leading us into the following scene. His music struck just the right mixture of grand guignol, high tragedy, and tongue-in-cheek humor, opera, and techno. It led the audience into the play and kept them engaged at every turn. The moments of Britten and Verdi specifically called for in the script are my directions, and Daniel made great use of the recordings we had, integrating them seamlessly into the action and interpolating his music and theirs so that it felt like the music was all from the same world.

Masks. The play is suffused with imagery of role-playing, masks, masques, plays, and themes of two-sidedness and hypocrisy. The opening masque can help establish those things very powerfully, as well as start to tell the story of the play and introduce the audience to the style of the production. In New York, Emily DeCola created an amazing number of detailed masks, using animal imagery, Warhol and Versace as inspirations. Each character had a specific relationship to his/her mask (e.g., Antonio was a white wolf, etc.). On one side the masks were white, and on the other side, they were full color. The skull masks we used referenced the Mexican "Day of the Dead" imagery, but were very stark in comparison to the opening.

Dance/Movement. In New York, Tracy Bersley did some amazing work on the two dances. At the opening, the actors were all robed in black swishy-stretchy fabric that Clint Ramos designed. They were all onstage as the red curtains parted, but it just looked like a black void. Slowly the white mask-faces emerged and then they switched to color faces, and then back. And then the orgy began, ending in a horrific rape of Lucretia. It was very effective. The masque of revengers referenced samurai warriors as well as Mexican Day of the Dead dancing skeletons. You need to cast people who can really move. Movement in the play is vital and expressionistic, never "dancey" — this should be dance for actors who can move. It should be visceral, meticulous, sexy. It's important that the movement carry the story forward at all times, but the dances and the murders are moments for the extremity of the world to really reach its fullest height of expression. The coronation can also be stylized movement. The second set of revenge masquers can certainly be comic.

Blood/Violence. Blood is necessary and should flow freely in any production of this play. Design costumes that are washable, stain-resistant and durable. Show as much as you can while leaving the audience's imagination to multiply it into a phantasmagoria of stage violence and mayhem. It is possible to do this without sacrificing the text or the story. Don't add gratuitous moments — there are plenty embedded in the text and tale itself. Get someone really, really good at stage violence to work with you; keep the text and the story at the forefront, but don't be squeamish — the violence should be outrageous, and never repetitive. The fight at the end of Act One should be horrifically realistic and explosive. The murders at the banquet can be a little more stylized and theatrical. All the violence needs to be both horrible and entertaining, and should never repeat itself. Each thing should surprise. The quick killings of Spurio, Ambitioso, and Supervacuo are certainly comic, but they should be no less bloody or real. When we shot Vindice in New York, his blood splattered all over that big mirror. It got a good reaction. When Hippolito and Vindice were setting up the Duke's dead body in Act Two, Scene 7, they have to bend an arm in rigor mortis in order to lean him on it — make sure to have a good live cracking/crunching sound for this moment. It was our one guaranteed laugh in New York. We used a cheap plastic cocktail glass, and it worked amazingly well.

17

You will want one person to be in charge of blood and blood effects — it's a big job on this play. You need to cast people with super-solid stage combat experience. Get the fight director, blood maker, properties designer, and costume designer together early in the process to hash it all out.

Props. The key prop is Gloriana. The skull has to be realistic and durable. It also has to fit snugly, but not too tightly on the finial of the dress form. The dress form needs to be on wheels that roll smoothly and quietly. The dress form should be used in Act One, Scene 5, where both Castiza and Gratiana can attach items to it. This should be the same one Vindice uses in Act One, Scene 11. He dresses her in a cloak that Hippolito can get under and hide completely beneath. It works best if he can get his arms out around the sides. In New York, Haynes Thigpen as Hippolito was quite hilarious, holding out a fan and smacking the Duke's hand when he reached out to touch her. At this point, she should be wearing a mask, similar to one of the prologue masks, and a veil over her head. The Duke simply lifts the mask and starts kissing and licking the skull before he realizes what she is.

Weapons. There's a lot of them. The eight swords at the end should all be identical and conjure up kabuki or samurai warriors. Make sure to have a meeting early on with the director, costume designer, blood maker, and fight director to get the weaponry started.

TEXT

The play is mostly in verse, and that should be respected. It often has a naturally jagged style that allows the dialogue to sound contemporary without extra effort. Good clear speech is necessary, but it need not be overdone. The iambic rhythms should be fully honored, and words — would that this need not be said — should not be changed.

ADAPTATION

Please read the original text. This version is an adaptation of that, and it is an honest attempt to bring the play forward to a contemporary audience in an accessible, respectful way. I recommend the New Mermaids edition by Brian Gibbons. The Revels edition by R.A. Foakes is also good.

What did I do to the original text?

The three major things done were:

1) A ton of editing, interpolating, and streamlining.

2) Changed Castiza's story line. I felt for Castiza to stay at home as a good chaste daughter after Piato's visit rang false. I also felt that it was important for Vindice's actions at home to have some consequences, even if he never knows what they are.

3) Created a fuller story for Antonio and Pietro. In the original there is very little about Antonio. I wanted to explore what the alternative rule of Antonio would be and what kind of a world Vindice was helping to create. The notion was that this play would be the tragedy to end all tragedies, and that in a world ruled by the puritan Antonio, such bloody and lustful business would be over — or would at least happen only behind closed doors. No more tragedy, no more fun.

Who wrote what lines? Webster, Marston, Bacon, Berger, etc? It's not important. If you really want to know or have a good dramaturg with lots of time on his or her hands, have fun figuring it out! However, it should (I hope) feel like a play by one author, even though it was written by a bunch of people unknowingly collaborating over four hundred years.

STAGE DIRECTIONS

The stage directions included in this text are specific indicators about how the play has worked in the past. I have deliberately kept the directions sparse, so as to allow future directors and actors the ability to reinvent this work according to their own imagination. However, ignoring the directions per se is not recommended.

DOUBLING

This version of the play was written to be performed by nineteen actors, with the actor playing Flaminio also playing Spurio's Servant, and the Officers occasionally doubling as Attendants.

Any number of people or doubling scenarios may be used in future productions as long as the overall consistency of tone and story is kept clear.

PLAY

Whatever you do, don't make the play too serious. It must dance in the graveyard. Have fun, be creative, and share the story with clarity at every point. There are no internal moments that are not fully engaged with the audience.

Whatever you do, don't make the play too comic. It must be based in real motivations and behavior pushed to extremes. It could easily be played as pure camp or simply a send-up of Shakespearean conventions. That will tire you and your audience out early — it needs to have a sincerity of purpose and full heart of truth.

Whatever you do, have a good time working on this play. It is a play in love with playmaking and the theater. And it's one of a kind — enjoy!

—Jesse Berger
New York City
February 2006

CHARACTERS

DUKE of Venice

DUCHESS of Venice

LUSSURIOSO, the Duke's son and heir

SPURIO, a bastard of the Duke's

AMBITIOSO, eldest son to the Duchess

SUPERVACUO, middle son to the Duchess

FLAMINIO, youngest son to the Duchess

VINDICE, a revenger, called Piato in disguise

HIPPOLITO, his brother, in Lussurioso's service

CASTIZA, their sister

GRATIANA, their mother, a dressmaker

ANTONIO, a powerful lord of law

LUCRETIA, his wife

PIETRO, a lord and friend to Antonio

NENCIO, a lord in service to Lussurioso

SORDIDO, a lord in service to Lussurioso

ANTONIO'S LORD

SPURIO'S SERVANT

FIRST OFFICER

Officers, Lords, and Servants of the Court

There is no heaven but revenge.

—*Thomas Nashe*

THE REVENGER'S TRAGEDY

ACT ONE

Prologue

Music. Red curtains open. Vindice greets the audience. He disappears as the company is revealed, all wearing two-sided masks. The court of Venice. Revels, a masque. A dance, in which Lucretia, Antonio's wife, is raped by Flaminio, the Duchess' youngest son. Company frieze: Duke, Lussurioso his son, Spurio his bastard, Duchess and her sons Ambitioso, Supervacuo and Flaminio. Reenter Vindice.

Scene 1

Cemetery.

VINDICE.
  Duke: royal lecher; go, gray-haired adultery;
  And thou his son as impious steeped as he,
  And thou his bastard true-begot in evil,
  And thou his Duchess that will do with devil;
  Four excellent characters! And here her brood:
  Vain, superfluous; rashful and ambitious —
  And this, her youngest cur, a rabid rapist.
(Exit court, except Duke.)

But he above all — O that marrowless age
Would stuff the hollow bones with damned desires
And 'stead of heat, kindle infernal fires
Within the spendthrift veins of a dry Duke,
A parched and juiceless luxur. O God, one
That has scarce blood enough to live upon
And he to riot like a son and heir?
O the thought of that
Turns my abusèd heartstrings into fret.

(Reveals skull of Gloriana.)

Thou shell of death, the once bright face of my
Betrothèd lady — my Gloriana —
When life and beauty filled these ragged imperfections,
When two angelic diamonds were set
In these unsightly rings — then twas a face
So far beyond the artificial shine
Of any woman's vainly bought complexion
That the uprightest man was bent with looking after her.
But O accursèd palace!
Thee, when thou wert appareled in thy flesh,
The old Duke poisoned

(Duke reappears.)

Because thy purer part would not consent
Unto his palsy-lust; for old men lustful
Do show like young men angry, eager-violent,
Outbid, like their limited performances.
Hum, who e'er knew a murder gone unpaid?
(To skull:) Believe me, I am nothing but your grave
And I shall keep your blessèd memory
Longer than a thousand epitaphs.
Vengeance, thou art murder's debtor, and thus
Must pay thine principle to tragedy;
O keep thy day, hour, minute, I beseech,
To those thou interest owe. *(To skull:)* Be merry, merry,
Advance thee, O thou terror to fat folks
To have their costly-covered flesh worn off
As bare as this; for banquets, ease and laughter
Can make great men, as greatness goes by clay,
But wise men little are more great than they.

(Duke disappears. Enter his brother Hippolito.)

HIPPOLITO.
　　Still sighing o'er death's visage?
VINDICE.
　　　　　　　　　　　　　　　　Brother, welcome!
　　What comfort bringst thou? How go things at court?
HIPPOLITO.
　　In silk and silver, brother, never braver.
VINDICE.
　　　　　　　　　　　　　　　　　Puh,
　　Hast any news, speak, are we happy yet?
　　Thy wrongs and mine are for one vengeance set.
HIPPOLITO.
　　It may prove happiness.
VINDICE.
　　　　　　　　　　　What ist may prove?
　　Give me to taste.
HIPPOLITO.
　　　　　　　　　Give me your hearing, then.
　　You know my place at court.
VINDICE.
　　　　　　　　　　　　Ay, the Duke's chamber.
HIPPOLITO.
　　Of late my duty waits upon his son
　　Lussurioso, heir of lust;
　　This the purpose: last evening unto this
　　The Duke's son warily enquired for me,
　　Conjuring me in private stealthily
　　To seek some strange digested fellow forth —
　　To give you the true word — some base-coined pandar.
VINDICE.
　　I reach you, for I know his heat is such,
　　Were there as many concubines as ladies
　　He would not be contained, he must fly out.
HIPPOLITO.
　　Brother, well and truly you've bespoke him —
　　He knows not you, but I'll swear you know him!
VINDICE.
　　I'll be a right man then, a man o'th'time
　　For to be honest is not to be i'th'world.
　　Brother, I'll be that strange composèd fellow.

HIPPOLITO.

Tis meet; and I'll present you to him, brother.

VINDICE.

Mayhap reveal occasion for revenge —
The small'st advantage fattens wrongèd men;
And courts are theaters, where some princes play,
Some slaves, all to one end and of one clay.

HIPPOLITO.

You must the part of pandar play disguised.

VINDICE.

I have a costume that will fit it bawdly —

(Enter Gratiana and Castiza.)

Here comes our mother.

HIPPOLITO.

                    And sister.

VINDICE.

                            We must feign.

GRATIANA.

What news from court, Hippolito?

HIPPOLITO.

Tis whispered there the Duchess' youngest son
Has played a rape on lord Antonio's wife.

GRATIANA.

On that religious lady! Royal blood!

CASTIZA.

Monster! He deserves to die.

VINDICE.

Sister, y'ave sentenced most direct, and true.
Mother, I must take leave of you.

GRATIANA.

                        Wherefore?

VINDICE.

With speedy haste I fly unto the court.

HIPPOLITO.

That he does.

GRATIANA.

          Speedy indeed!

CASTIZA.

                Must you leave?

VINDICE.

Faith, dear sister, I must.

For since our worthy father's funeral
My life's unnatural to me, e'en compelled,
As if I lived now when I should be dead.
GRATIANA.
Indeed he was a worthy gentleman
Had his estate been fellow to his mind.
VINDICE.
The Duke did much deject him.
GRATIANA.

Much.

VINDICE.

Too much.

And through disgrace oft smothered in his spirit
When it would mount. Sure I think he died
Of discontent, the politician's plague.
GRATIANA.
Most sure he did.
VINDICE.

Did he? 'Lack, you know all,

You were his midnight secretary.
GRATIANA.

No,

He was too wise to trust me with his thoughts.
VINDICE.
I'faith then, father thou wast wise indeed,
'Wives are but made to go to bed and feed.' —
O pardon, mother — I forgot: and sew.
HIPPOLITO.
Ha ha.
VINDICE.

Come mother, sister.

HIPPOLITO.

We must go.

VINDICE.
Farewell then both! You'll bring me onward, brother?
(Enter court.)
HIPPOLITO.
I will.
VINDICE.

I'll quickly turn into another.

(Exeunt.)

Scene 2

At the court: The Duke, Lussurioso his son, the Duchess, Spurio
the bastard, the Duchess' two sons Ambitioso and Supervacuo,
the third her youngest son Flaminio with Officers, Lussurioso's
lords Nencio and Sordido.

DUKE.
    Duchess: it is your youngest son, we're sorry;
    His violent act has e'en drawn blood of honor
    And stained the forehead of our state.
    Who dares now whisper
    That dares not soon speak out, and e'en proclaim
    With loud words and broad pens our closest shame.
    We sit in judgment; therefore tis our fate
    To live in fear and die to live in hate.
DUCHESS.
(Kneels.)
    My lord, be merciful:
    Think him to be your own as I am yours;
    Call him not son-in-law: the law I fear.
    Temper his fault with pity.
LUSSURIOSO.
                        Good my father,
    His crime wast beauty to admire o'ermuch
    Then let him but lose face, not yet his head.
AMBITIOSO.
    Beseech your grace, be soft and mild —
SUPERVACUO.
                         — Let not
    Relentless law fall down upon our brother.
SPURIO.
(Aside.)
    He yields small comfort yet — hope he shall die —
    And if a bastard's wish might stand in force,
    Would all the court were turned into a corpse.
(Enter Antonio, Lucretia, Pietro and Antonio's Lord.)

DUCHESS.

No pity yet! Must I rise fruitless then — ?

ANTONIO.

My honored Duke, let not light flatteries
O'erweigh the sacred scales of law.
Justice alone prevails beyond the grave,
Her eyes like holy beacons scan our lives.
If this doth fail to move you sir, O hear
My virtuous wife, speechless in her ravishment.

(Lucretia attempts to speak but collaspses in tears into Antonio's arms.)

PIETRO.

A rape! Why tis the very core of lust,
Double adultery.

FLAMINIO.

          So sir.

PIETRO.

               And which was worse —

DUKE.

A rape, upon good lord Antonio's wife,
That general honest lady. Confess, my boy:
What moved you to't?

FLAMINIO.

              Why flesh and blood, my lord:
What should move men unto a woman else?

LUSSURIOSO.

Mock not thy doom; I love thee thus far
(Though marriage only has made thee my brother)
To advise thee.

DUCHESS.

          Play not with thy death.

FLAMINIO.

I thank you troth, good admonitions faith.

DUCHESS.

If you'd the grace now to make use of them.

PIETRO.

What can be said i'defense of such an act?

FLAMINIO.

Well then tis done, and it would please me well
Were it to do again. Sure she's a goddess
For I'd no power to see her and to live;
If I must die, her beauty's then my scaffold.

And yet methinks I might be granted stay:
My fault being sport, let me but die in play.

DUKE.

His fault was sweet sport which the world approves;
Shalt die for that which every woman loves?

ANTONIO.

The law, my lord, demands his sudden death.

DUKE.

Impartial doom shall take fast hold of his
Unclean attempt.

DUCHESS.

O what it is to have an old-cool Duke
To be as slack in tongue as in performance.

DUKE.

We will defer the judgment till next sitting!

SPURIO.

(Aside.)

Pox on't, what makes my Dad stop now?

DUKE.

In the meantime let him be kept close prisoner.

(Exit Lucretia, screaming.)

ANTONIO.

My liege!

PIETRO.

       I must protest —

DUKE.

               We have spoken.

(Exit Duke, Lussurioso one way, Antonio, Pietro another.)

SPURIO.

(Aside.)

Delayed, deferred, nay then if judgment have
Cold blood, flattery and bribes will kill it.

(Exit.)

AMBITIOSO.

(To Flaminio.)

Brother, this makes for thee.

SUPERVACUO.

Fear not, we'll have a trick to set thee free.

FLAMINIO.

In that hope I rest.

SUPERVACUO.

                Farewell, be merry.

FLAMINIO.

  Ay, if I could but die in jest!

(Exit Supervacuo, Ambitioso one way, Flaminio guarded by Officers another.)

DUCHESS.

  Wast ever known step-Duchess was so mild
  And calm as I? Some now would plot his death
  And make his withered grace fall to his grave.
  Some second wife would do this, and dispatch
  Her double-loathèd lord at meat and sleep.
  Indeed tis true an old man's twice a child,
  Mine cannot speak! One of his single words
  Would quite have freed my youngest dearest son
  From death or durance; and yet spake he not.
  Well, therefore wedlock faith shall be forgot!
  I'll kill him in his forehead, hate there feed —
  That wound is deepest though it never bleed.

(Enter Spurio.)

  And here comes he whom my heart points unto,
  His bastard son, but my love's true-begot —
  Many a fecund letter have I sent him
  Swelled up with jewels, and the timorous man
  Is but coldly kind to my hot advance —
  H'as spied me now.

SPURIO.

                Madam? Your grace so private?

  My duty on your hand.

DUCHESS.

  Upon my hand, sir; troth I think you'd fear
  To kiss my hand too if my lip stood there.

SPURIO.

  Witness I would not, madam.

(Kisses her.)

DUCHESS.

                Tis a wonder:

  It is as easy way unto a Duchess
  As to a common dame, if her love answer.
  What have you thought of me?

SPURIO.

    Madam, I ever think of you in duty,
    Regard and —

DUCHESS.

                      Puh, upon my love I mean.

SPURIO.

    I would twere love, but t'as a fouler name
    Than lust; you are my father's wife, your grace may guess now
    What I would call it.

DUCHESS.

                  Why thou art his son but falsely,
    Tis a hard question whether he begot thee.

SPURIO.

    I'faith tis true: I'm an uncertain man of more uncertain woman.
    Maybe twas his groom o'th'stable begot me, as well as any —
    puh, you know I know not — Marry, he could ride a horse well,
    a quickly gallop!

DUCHESS.

    Nay, set you a horseback once, you'll ne'er light off.

SPURIO.

    Indeed I am for wild and night-long rides.

DUCHESS.

    That's more the sign thou art of royal blood.
    Let it stand firm both in thy thought and mind
    That the Duke was thy father; why thy injury
    Is th'more: for had he cut thee a right diamond,
    Thou hadst been next set in the Dukedom's ring.
    What wrong can equal this? Canst thou be tame
    And think upon't?

SPURIO.

                No, mad and think upon't.

DUCHESS.

    O what a grief tis that a man should live
    But once i'th'world, and then to live a bastard,
    Half damned i'th'conception.

SPURIO.

                  Rather had I
    The devil to my father and did know him.

DUCHESS.

    Who but an eunuch would not sin, his bed
    By one false minute disinherited?

SPURIO.

(Aside.)

    Ay, there's the vengeance that my birth was wrapped in;
    I'll call foul incest but a venial sin.

DUCHESS.

    Cold still: in vain then must a Duchess woo?

SPURIO.

    Madam, I blush to say what I will do.

DUCHESS.

    Thence flew sweet comfort. Earnest, and farewell.

(They kiss.)

    Old Duke, our vengeance shall reach high on thee:
    We'll arm thy brow with shameless cuckoldry.

(Exit.)

SPURIO.

    How one incestuous kiss picks open hell.
    Duke, thou didst do me wrong and by thy act
    Adultery is my nature.
    Faith, if the truth were known, I was begot
    After some gluttonous dinner — some stirring dish
    Was my first father; when deep healths went round
    And ladies' cheeks were painted red with wine,
    Their tongues as short and nimble as their heels
    Uttering words sweet and thick, and when they rose
    Were merrily disposed to fall again.
    In such a whispering and withdrawing hour
    Was I stolen softly — O damnation met
    The sin of feasts, drunken adultery.
    I was begot in impudent wine and lust;
    I feel it swell me, my revenge is just.
    Stepmother, I consent to thy desires,
    I love thy mischief well. But I hate thee —
    And those three curs thy sons, wishing confusion,
    Death and disgrace may be their epitaphs.
    As for my brother, the Duke's 'only son,'

(Enter Lussurioso.)

    Whose birth is more beholding to report
    Than mine, and yet perhaps as falsely sown,
    I'll loose my days upon him; hate all I!
    Duke, on thy brow I'll draw a bastard's smile:
    A bastard should make cuckolds by his nature,

Sith he is the son of a cuckold-maker.
(Exeunt.)

Scene 3

Lussurioso's chambers: Lussurioso being bathed or massaged by Nencio and Sordido, Hippolito attending. Enter Vindice in disguise as Piato.

VINDICE.
What, brother, am I far enough from myself?
HIPPOLITO.
As if another man had been sent whole
Into the world.
VINDICE.
    It will confirm me bold —
The child o'th'court — let blushes dwell i'th'country.
(Lussurioso is toweled and oiled by Nencio and Sordido.)
HIPPOLITO.
Sfoot, the Duke's son! Settle your looks.
VINDICE.
Let me not be doubted.
HIPPOLITO.
My lord.
LUSSURIOSO.
Hippolito, I am in heat impatient —
Hast brought a balm to soothe this burning?
HIPPOLITO.
        Sir,
After deep search, I made choice of yon fellow —
Whom I guess rare for many hot employments:
This our luxurious age doth swim in him;
He's like a brother to this present minute.
LUSSURIOSO.
We thank thee.
(Gives silver coin.)

HIPPOLITO.
Your plenteous honor — an excellent fellow, my lord.
LUSSURIOSO.
So, give us leave —
(Exit Hippolito, Nencio, Sordido. To Vindice:)
Welcome, be not far off,
We must be better acquainted — Push, be bold
With us, thy hand.
VINDICE.
With all my heart, i'faith!
(Applying lotion.)
How dost sweet skin? When shall we lie together?
LUSSURIOSO.
I can forget myself in private, friend,
But elsewhere do you remember me.
VINDICE.
O
Very well sir — I conster myself saucy!
LUSSURIOSO.
What art thou called?
VINDICE.
Piato, so please my lord.
LUSSURIOSO.
What hast been? — of what profession?
VINDICE.
A bonesetter.
LUSSURIOSO.
A bonesetter!
VINDICE.
A bawd my lord.
One that sets bones together.
LUSSURIOSO.
Thou hast been scrivener to much knavery then?
VINDICE.
Full to abundance, sir; I have been witness
To the surrenders of a thousand virgins.
LUSSURIOSO.
Then thou knowst in the world strange lust?
VINDICE.
O fulsome lust!
Drunken procreation, which begets many drunkards;

Some father dreads not, gone to bed in wine
To slide from th'mother and slip unto th'daughter;
Some uncles are adulterous with their nieces,
Brothers with brothers' wives — O the hour of incest!
Any kin now next to the rim o'th'sister
Is man's meat in these days —

LUSSURIOSO.

                                    In troth it is;
But let this talk glide. Now wert thou as secret
As experienced, I would embrace thee with
Employment near and thou shouldst swell in money.

VINDICE.

Secret? I ne'er had that disease o'th'mother,
I praise my father! Why are men made closed
But to keep thoughts in best? I tell you: put
Some secret in a woman overnight,
Your doctor may find it swimming i'th'urinal
I'th'morning!

LUSSURIOSO.

                        So thou'rt confirmed in me
And thus I enter thee.
(Gives silver coin.)

VINDICE.

                                This silver devil
Will quickly enter any man; come in!

LUSSURIOSO.

Attend me, I am past my depth in lust
And I must swim or drown. All my desires
Are leveled at a virgin close to court;
I have conveyed her many amorous lines
And jewels to ravish her: all which and more
She, foolish-chaste, sent back.

VINDICE.

                                    Ist possible?
If your desires be such, she so resistant,
In troth my lord, I'd be revenged and marry her.

LUSSURIOSO.

Push, the dowry of her blood and her fortunes
Are both too mean — good enough to be bad withal.
Give me my bed by stealth — there's true delight —
What breeds a loathing in't but night by night?

VINDICE.

A very fine religion!

LUSSURIOSO.

Therefore thus:

Go thou and with a smooth enchanting tongue
Bewitch her ears and cozen her of grace;
Purchase her honor, which she calls honesty;
Bring me its first expense, her chastity.

VINDICE.

Make known the lady to me and my brain
Shall swell with strange invention.

LUSSURIOSO.

She I mean

Is th'only daughter to Madam Gratiana,
The late widow.

(Pours glass of wine.)

VINDICE.

(Aside.)

O my sister, my sister!

LUSSURIOSO.

Why dost walk aside?

VINDICE.

My lord, I was thinking how I might begin,
As thus — "Oh lady" —

LUSSURIOSO.

Dost know the daughter then?

VINDICE.

O excellent well by sight.

LUSSURIOSO.

That was her brother

That did prefer thee to us.

VINDICE.

Is it so?

I knew I had seen him somewhere.

LUSSURIOSO.

And therefore prithee let thy heart to him
Be as a virgin, closed.

VINDICE.

O my good lord.

LUSSURIOSO.

We may laugh at that ignorance within him.

(Laughs.)
VINDICE.
(Aside:)
    A pretty-perfumed villain!
LUSSURIOSO.

                              I've bethought me:
    If she prove chaste still and immovable,
    Venture upon the mother, and with gold
    As I will furnish thee, begin with her.
VINDICE.
    O fie, that's the wrong end, my lord. Tis mere
    Impossible a mother by any gold
    Should turn bawd unto her virgin daughter!
LUSSURIOSO.
    Why tis now no exotic dish, such bawds
    Are so in league with women nowadays
    They do eclipse three-quarters of all mothers.
VINDICE.
    Let me alone then to eclipse the fourth.
LUSSURIOSO.
    Why, well said; come, I'll furnish thee: but first
    Swear to be true in all.
VINDICE.

                    True?

LUSSURIOSO.

                        Nay, but swear!

VINDICE.
    I hope your honor little doubts my faith.
LUSSURIOSO.
    Yet, for my humor's sake, cause I love swearing.
VINDICE.
    Cause you love swearing, 'slud I will.
(Swears on wine.)
LUSSURIOSO.

                              Enough.

    Ere long look to be made of better stuff.
(Exit.)
VINDICE.
(Spits out wine.)
    O!
    Now let me burst, I've eaten noble poison!

Swear me to foul my sister! Binding oath!
Sister, I durst make a promise of him to thee:
I shalt dis-heir him; it shall be thine honor.
Yet, twould not prove the meanest policy
In this disguise to try the faith of both.
Another might have had the self-same office,
Some slave that would have wrought effectually,
Ay, and perhaps o'erwrought 'em: therefore I
Will apply myself to forget my nature,
As if no part of me were kin to 'em,
So touch 'em — though I durst almost for good
Lay my lands in heaven upon their blood.
(Exeunt.)

Scene 4

Antonio's apartments. Britten's The Rape of Lucretia. *Lucretia enters to a chaise and a small table. She drinks poison in a glass of wine, lies down, and then stabs herself. Dies. Enter Antonio, discovering her dead body.*

ANTONIO.
    — Hast thou undone thyself?
    A loathsome sight — O cruel to leave me thus!
    Thy lips hath color still — Shall I lay one
    Last kiss upon them? One, and then no more.
(Kisses her.)
    What's this? Sour taste of acid? Poison then!
    I'll risk a drop to touch thy lips again.
(Enter Pietro, Hippolito, and Antonio's Lord.)
PIETRO.
    O foul —
ANTONIO.
           Draw near and witness: violent rape
    Has played a glorious act: behold, my lords,
    A sight that strikes man out of me.

PIETRO.

That virtuous lady.

HIPPOLITO.

Precedent for wives.

ANTONIO.

Dead!

HIPPOLITO.

We have grief too that yet walks without tongue.

PIETRO.

Lesser cares can speak, greater cares are silent.

ANTONIO.

You deal with truth, my lord. I will not swell
Like a tragedian in forcèd passion
Of affected strains. She, her honor forced,
Deemed it a nobler dowry for her name
To die with poison than to live with shame.

LORD.

A wondrous lady of rare fire compact.

HIPPOLITO.

What judgment follows the offenders back?

LORD.

Faith, none my lord, it cools and is deferred.

HIPPOLITO.

Delay the doom for rape?

PIETRO.

But note who tis should die —
The Duchess' son. The Duke will be a saver:
Judgment in this age is family to favor.

HIPPOLITO.

Here I do take my oath upon her blood:
If judgment speaks in gold and spares the life
Of such a serpent, e'en before their eyes
I'll let his soul out.

PIETRO.

Sir, you speak my thoughts
And I do double on thy oath with mine.

ANTONIO.

God hath engrossed all justice in his hands
And there is none but comes from him.

HIPPOLITO.

Twere pity

The ruins of so fair a monument
Should not be dipped in the defacers' blood.
PIETRO.
No doubt our grief and yours may one day court it
When we are more familiar with revenge.
ANTONIO.
Tis justice wild thou dost espouse;
The more man's nature runs to vengeance,
The more ought law to weed it out.
PIETRO.
Thou knowst the Dukedom is corrupt.
ANTONIO.
I will pursue revenge in court!
If th'law do justice fail, I'll not fail the law.
God's my comfort, gentlemen, and I joy
In this one happiness above the waste,
That being an honest man I'd a wife so chaste.
(Exeunt.)

Scene 5

Gratiana's household, a dressmaker's shop. Castiza the sister discovered, dressing a dress form.

CASTIZA.
How hardly shall that maiden be beset
Whose only fortunes are her constant thoughts,
That has no other child's-part but her honor
That keeps her low and empty in estate.
Maids and their honors are like poor beginners;
Were not sin rich, there would be fewer sinners.
Why had not virtue a revènue? Well,
I know the cause: twould have impoverished hell.
(Enter Vindice her brother disguised as Piato.)
VINDICE.
Lady, the best wishes to your sex:
Fair skin and new gowns.

(Gives letter.)
CASTIZA.

O they shall thank you, sir —

Whence this?
VINDICE.

O from a dear and worthy friend,

Mighty!
CASTIZA.

From whom?
VINDICE.

The Duke's son.
CASTIZA.

Receive that!

(Slaps him.)
I swore I would put anger in my hand
To him that next appeared in that base office
To be his sin's attorney. Bear to him
That figure of my hate upon thy cheek
Whilst tis yet hot, and I will thank thee for't;
Tell him my honor shall have a rich name
When several harlots shall share his with shame.
Farewell, commend me to him in my hate!
(Exit.)
VINDICE.
Sister, were I myself, I'd kiss thee straight!
It is not in the power of words to taint thee.
Yet still for the salvation of my soul,
Sith I swore an oath to this, I will lay
Hard siege unto my mother, though I know
A siren's tongue could not bewitch her so.
(Enter Gratiana.)
Mass, fitly, here she comes:
(Replaces disguise.)
Madam, good afternoon.
GRATIANA.

Y'are welcome, sir.
VINDICE.
The city's heir commends himself to you:
The Duke's son.
GRATIANA.

I'm much honored that he pleases

To rank me in his thoughts.

VINDICE.

So are you, lady:
One that is like to be our sudden Duke;
How blest were they now that could pleasure him
E'en with anything almost. That young Duke
Has long desired your daughter.

GRATIANA.

— Desired?

VINDICE.

Therefore be wise; I speak as more a friend
To you than him. Madam, I know you're poor:
There are too many poor ladies already;
Should you increase the number? Tis despised.
Live wealthy, rightly understand the world
And chide away that foolish country girl
Keeps company with your daughter: chastity.

GRATIANA.

Fie, the riches of the world cannot hire
A mother t'such a most unnatural task.

VINDICE.

No, but a thousand silver pieces can.

(Offers silver coins.)

There will be fools still I perceive, still fools.
Would I be poor, dejected, scorned of greatness,
Swept from the palace, and see other daughters
Spring with the dew o'th'court, having mine own
So much desired and loved — by the Duke's son?
No, I would raise my state upon her breast,
Take coach upon her lip, and all her parts
Should keep men after men and I would ride
In pleasure upon pleasure.

(Gives silver coins.)

You brought her forth, she may well bring you home.

GRATIANA.

O heavens, this overcomes me!

VINDICE.

Already?

GRATIANA.

(Aside.)

He touched me nearly, made my virtues bate

45

When his tongue struck upon my poor estate.

VINDICE.

What think you now lady, speak, are you wiser?
What said advancement to you? Thus it said:
The daughter's fall lifts up the mother's head!
Tis no shame to be bad, because tis common.

GRATIANA.

Ay, that's the comfort on't.

VINDICE.

(Aside.)

The comfort on't!

I keep the best for last —
(Drops gold coins.)

GRATIANA.

Ay, these are they —

VINDICE.

O!

GRATIANA.

— that would raise our state perpetual riches!
I blush to think what for your sakes I'll do.

VINDICE.

(Aside.)

O suffering heaven, turn the precious side
Of both mine eyeballs inward, not to see myself.

GRATIANA.

Look you, sir.

VINDICE.

Holla.

GRATIANA.

Let this thank your pains.

(Kisses him.)

VINDICE.

O you're a kind madam.

GRATIANA.

I'll see how I can move.

VINDICE.

Your words will sting.

GRATIANA.

If she be still chaste I'll ne'er call her mine.

VINDICE.

That woman is all male whom none can enter.

(Enter Castiza.)

CASTIZA.
 Madam, what makes yon evil-officed man
 In presence of you?

GRATIANA.
                    Why?

CASTIZA.
                              He lately brought
 Immodest writing sent from the Duke's son
 To tempt me to dishonorable act.

GRATIANA.
 Dishonorable act? Good honorable fool,
 That wouldst be honest cause thou wouldst be so,
 Producing not one reason but thy will;
 And t'as a good report, prettily commended —
 But pray by whom? Mean people, ignorant people!
 The better sort I'm sure cannot abide it.
 And by what rule should we square out our lives
 But by our betters' actions? If thou knewst
 What twere to lose it, thou would never keep it:
 Virginity is paradise locked up;
 You cannot come by yourself without fee,
 And twas decreed that man should keep the key.
 Deny advancement, treasure, the Duke's son!

CASTIZA.
 I cry you mercy, lady, I mistook you:
 Did you see my mother? Pray God I have not lost her.

GRATIANA.
 Are you as proud to me as coy to him?
 Do you not know me now?

CASTIZA.
                              Why, are you she?
 The world's so changed, one shape into another,
 Tis a wise child now that knows her mother.

GRATIANA.
 I owe your cheek my hand
 For that presumption now, but I'll forget it;
 Come, you shall leave those childish 'haviors,
 And understand your time; fortunes flow to you —
 What, will you be a girl?

CASTIZA.

                     Such words show not so well
  From out your mouth, better in his.

VINDICE.

                        I wonder
  Your own good mother's words will not be taken;
  For gold, virginity is oft forsaken.
  Tis honesty you urge: what's honesty?
  And what woman so foolish to keep honesty
  And be not able to keep herself? No,
  Blest are you: you have happiness alone;
  Others must fall to thousands, you to one,
  Sufficient in himself to make you dazzle
  The world with jewels —

GRATIANA.

                   O if I were young
  I should be ravished.

CASTIZA.

              Ay, to lose your honor.

VINDICE.

  His grace will add more honor to it by his title;
  Your mother will tell you how.

GRATIANA.

                That I will.

VINDICE.

  O think upon the pleasure of the palace,
  Securèd ease and state; the stirring meats
  Ready to move out of the dishes
  That e'en now quicken when they're eaten;
  Banquets abroad by torchlight, musics, sports,
  Nine coaches waiting — hurry, hurry, hurry —

CASTIZA.

  Ay, to the devil!

VINDICE.

            To th'Duke, by my faith!

GRATIANA.

  Ay, to the Duke. Daughter, you'd scorn to think
  On the devil an' you were once to court.

VINDICE.

  Who'd sit at home in a neglected room
  Dealing her short-lived beauty to the bible's pictures

That are as useless as old men, when those
Poorer in face and fortune than herself
Walk with a hundred acres on their backs?
Why are there so few honest women, but
Because tis a poor profession? All thrives but chastity!

GRATIANA.

Troth, he says true.

CASTIZA.

                        False! I defy you both!
Mother, come from that poisonous woman there.

GRATIANA.

Where?

CASTIZA.

Do you not see her? She's sewn too inward then:
Slave, perish in thy office! You heavens please
Henceforth to make the mother a disease
Which first begins with me! Yet I've outgrown you.

(Exit.)

GRATIANA.

Peevish, coy, foolish! But return this answer:
My lord shall be most welcome when his pleasure
Conducts him this way; I will sway mine own:
Women with women can work best alone.

(Exit.)

VINDICE.

Indeed I'll tell him so.
Why does not heaven turn black or with a frown
Undo the world? Why does not earth start up
And strike the sins that tread upon it? O:

(Enter Castiza to mirror.)

Were't not for gold and women,
There would be no damnation.

(Enter Lussurioso.)

But twas decreed before the world began
That they should be the hooks to catch at man.

(Exeunt. Castiza removes her corset, disappearing as Lussurioso enters.)

Scene 6

Lussurioso's chambers. Enter Lussurioso to Vindice/Piato.

LUSSURIOSO.
  Piato.
VINDICE.
       My lord.
LUSSURIOSO.
           Delay not, say:
  Have I a pleasure toward?
VINDICE.
                O my lord.
LUSSURIOSO.
  Ravish me in thine answer: art thou rare,
  ·Is she a woman?
VINDICE.
           In all but in desire.
LUSSURIOSO.
  Then she's in nothing!
VINDICE.
              I durst undertake
  With half those words to flat a puritan's wife,
  But she is closed and good.
LUSSURIOSO.
             I never thought
  Their sex had been a wonder till this minute.
  But where comes in this comfort?
VINDICE.
                 In a fine place, my lord:
  The maid being dull, what did me? I straight
  Set spurs unto the mother; golden spurs!
LUSSURIOSO.
  What fruit from her?
VINDICE.
           The unnatural mother
  Did with her tongue so hard beset her honor

That the poor fool was struck to silent wonder;
Yet still the maid like an unlighted candle
Was cold and chaste. Constant, the girl departed,
But the good anxious madam, half mad, threw me
These promising words which I took deeply note of:
'My lord shall be most welcome' —
LUSSURIOSO.

                              Faith, I thank her!
VINDICE.
'When his pleasure conducts him this way' —
LUSSURIOSO.

                                       Ay,
That shall be soon, i'faith!
VINDICE.
                        'I will sway mine own' —
LUSSURIOSO.
She does the wiser, I commend her for't.
VINDICE.
'Women with women can work best alone.'
LUSSURIOSO.
By this light so they can; give 'em their due,
We men cannot compare in that.
VINDICE.
                            Tis true, sir.
LUSSURIOSO.
Now my desires are happy — think on her!
Thou art a precious fellow, faith I love thee,
Be wise and make it thy revènue: Beg! Leg!
(Vindice begs. Lussurioso gives him a gold coin.)
Soon then I'll visit her, and tis till then
A year in my desires. Farewell, attend,
Trust me with thy preferment.
(Exit.)
VINDICE.
                        My loved lord.
O shall I kill him o'th'backside now? No!
I'll pierce him to his face, he shall die looking on me.
Thy veins are swelled with lust, this shall unfill 'em!
Forgive me God to call my mother wicked,
I cannot honor her; by this I fear me
Her tongue has turned my sister into use.

I was a villain not to be forsworn
To this our lecherous heir, the Duke's son;
For lawyers, merchants, politicians all,
Count beneficial perjury a sin small.
It shall go hard but I will guard her honor wise
And keep her port sure, though I burst the banks with lies.
(Enter Hippolito.)
HIPPOLITO.
Brother, how goes the world? I would know news
Of you, but I have news to tell you.
VINDICE.

                               Wash
Mine ear with water clean, that now is drenched
In royal sewage to the brim. What ist?
HIPPOLITO.
Foul juices, hot knavery, yet may have use:
The vicious old Duke's worthily abused,
The pen of his bastard doth write him cuckold!
VINDICE.
His bastard?
HIPPOLITO.

                Believe it; he and the Duchess
By night meet in their linen, they've been seen
By stair-foot pandars.
VINDICE.

                   O sin foul and deep!
(Enter Spurio and his Servant apart.)
HIPPOLITO.
See, see, there goes the bastard Spurio —
VINDICE.
Monstrous luxur!
(Spurio and Servant exit separately.)
Mark, there, there, that step! Now he's to the Duchess' bed;
Raise a banner, proclaim it thus:
Tis now the very reign of lust!
Whores are breeding and cuckolds are a-coining,
Apace, apace, apace, apace!
HIPPOLITO.
You flow well, brother.

VINDICE.

       Puh, I'm shallow yet,
Too sparing and too modest; shall I tell thee,
If every trick were told that's dealt by night
There are few here that would not blush outright.

HIPPOLITO.

 I am of that belief too.

(Enter Lussurioso.)

VINDICE.

       Who's this comes?

HIPPOLITO.

 The Duke's son!

VINDICE.

      Brother, fall back.

(Hippolito withdraws.)

 My lord.

LUSSURIOSO.

    Piato! Good, come now attend:
I do embrace this evening for the fittest
To taste of that young lady's early fruit.
Come, only thou and I.

VINDICE.

      My lord, my lord.

LUSSURIOSO.

 Why dost thou stop us?

VINDICE.

       I'd almost forgot —
The bastard! The bastard —

LUSSURIOSO.

      What of him?

VINDICE.

 This night, this hour — this minute, now —

LUSSURIOSO.

         What, what?

VINDICE.

 Shadows the Duchess —

LUSSURIOSO.

      Horrible word.

VINDICE.

 And like strong poison eats with his foul pen
Into the Duke your father's forehead.

LUSSURIOSO.

                O!

VINDICE.

This is the fruit of two beds.

(Music.)

LUSSURIOSO.

            I am mad.

VINDICE.

That passage he trod warily.

LUSSURIOSO.

           He did?

VINDICE.

And hushed his villain every step he took.

LUSSURIOSO.

His villain! I'll confound him.

VINDICE.

          Take 'em finely.

LUSSURIOSO.

I'll choke the issue of his wretched ink
Afore the bastard dare to spill a drop
Within my father's sheets! Come now, Piato!

(Enter bed. Exit Lussurioso and Vindice.)

HIPPOLITO.

Happy, swift; the court's a wildfire at midnight!
I'll follow the event.

(Exeunt.)

Scene 7

Bedchamber of the Duchess. Discover the Duke and Duchess having sex, silhouetted on a curtained bed. Enter Lussurioso with Vindice disguised.

LUSSURIOSO.

        There's the bastard!

VINDICE.

Softly, my lord, and you may take 'em twisted.

LUSSURIOSO.
    I care not how!
VINDICE.
                          O twill be glorious
To kill 'em doubled, when they're heaped —
LUSSURIOSO.
                                        Away!
    My spleen is not so lazy — Villain! Strumpet!
(Lussurioso tears the bed-curtain down, attacking the Duke.)
DUKE.
    Guard defend us!
DUCHESS.
                    Treason, treason!
DUKE.
(Kneeling.)
    O take me not in sleep,
    I have great sins, I must have days to pray;
    Nay, months, dear son, with penitential heaves,
    To lift 'em out and not to die unclear.
LUSSURIOSO.
    I am amazed to death.
DUKE.
                  Nay, villain, traitor,
(Grabs Lussurioso.)
    I'll grip thee with the nerves of wrath, and throw
    Thy head amongst the lawyers. Guard! Raise th'lights there!
(Enter Nencio, Sordido, Ambitioso, Supervacuo, Hippolito and Officers.)
OFFICER.
    How comes the quiet of your grace disturbed?
(Duchess dresses.)
DUKE.
    This boy that should be myself after me
    Would be myself before me, and in heat
    Of that ambition bloodily rushed in
    Intending to depose me in my bed.
SORDIDO.
    Duty and natural loyalty forfend!
(Officers hold Lussurioso.)
DUCHESS.
    He named us for a villain and a strumpet,
    A word that I abhor to 'file my lips with.

AMBITIOSO.

That was not so well-done, brother!

LUSSURIOSO.

I am abused!

VINDICE.

(Aside to Hippolito.)

Tis now good policy to be from sight.

HIPPOLITO.

I little dreamt his father slept here.

VINDICE.

O,

But since it fell so — would he had killed him!

(Exit Vindice and Hippolito stealthily.)

DUKE.

Be comforted, our Duchess, he shall die.

LUSSURIOSO.

Where's this slave Piato now? Out of mine eye,
Guilty of this abuse.

(Enter Spurio, dagger drawn.)

SPURIO.

Is the day out o'th'socket,

That it is noon at midnight, the court up?

LUSSURIOSO.

The bastard here!

Nay then, the truth of my intent shall out —
My lord and father, hear me —

DUKE.

Bear him hence.

LUSSURIOSO.

I can with loyalty excuse —

DUKE.

Excuse? To prison with the villain:
Death shall not long lag after him.

SPURIO.

(Aside.)

Good i'faith, then tis not much amiss.

LUSSURIOSO.

Brothers, my best release lies on your tongues.

AMBITIOSO.

It is our duties —

SUPERVACUO.

                — We'll sweat in pleading.

LUSSURIOSO.

An' if I'm freed to be my father's son

Again, then I may live to thank you both.

(Exit Lussurioso under guard of Officers.)

AMBITIOSO.

Now, brother, let our hate and love be woven

So subtly together that by speaking

One word for his life, make three for his death.

SUPERVACUO.

Set on, I'll not be far behind in breath.

DUKE.

(To Duchess.)

Ist possible my son should be so treacherous,

With vengeful blade to threat his father's life?

DUCHESS.

Tis most unfilial and foul, my love.

AMBITIOSO.

My gracious lord —

SUPERVACUO.

                Take pity.

DUKE.

                  Pity, boys?

AMBITIOSO.

Nay, we know the trespass is unpardonable —

SPURIO.

Base, wicked, unnatural.

DUCHESS.

           So it is.

SUPERVACUO.

In a son, O monstrous!

AMBITIOSO.

              We must confess

Some fathers would have sounded execution

With deadly-pointed haste —

SUPERVACUO.

             But my lord

Your grace may live the wonder of all times

In pardoning that offense which never yet

Had face to beg a pardon.

DUKE.

                                Honey, how's this?

DUCHESS.

Boys, be not so bold.

SPURIO.

                         Give justice course.

AMBITIOSO.

Forgive him, good my lord, he's your own son,
Yet — I must needs say — twas the viler done.

SUPERVACUO.

He's the next heir; yet this true reason gathers:
None can possess that dispossess their fathers.
Be merciful —

AMBITIOSO.

                Although —

DUKE.

                          You have prevailed,
My wrath like flaming wax hath spent itself:
(To Spurio:)
Go, let him be released.

SPURIO.

                   Indeed, my father.

SUPERVACUO.
(Aside to Ambitioso.)

Sfoot, how now, brother?

AMBITIOSO.
(Aside to Supervacuo.)

                  We must quickly turn.

DUCHESS.

Is this to be? His trespass left unpunished,
Yet my youngest son in jail doth languish?

SPURIO.

Come, with Lussurioso we shall speak,
And know the reason for his fault extreme.

DUKE.

Hie thee to his release!

DUCHESS.

                 With all good speed.
(Exit Spurio and Duchess.)

DUKE.

Well then. What boys, would you more grace of me?

AMBITIOSO.
　Your grace hath pleased to speak beside your spleen;
　I would it were so happy.
DUKE.
　　　　　　　　　Why, he's free.
SUPERVACUO.
　O my lord, the fault is too inhuman,
　Rather by all men's voices worthy death.
DUKE.
　Tis true too. Go put stop unto my bastard.
　And here receive this signet: doom shall pass.
　Direct it to the judges. He shall die —
　Ere many days — make haste.
AMBITIOSO.
　　　　　　　　　　All speed that may be.
SUPERVACUO.
　We could have wished his burden not so sore.
AMBITIOSO.
　We knew your grace did but delay before.
(Exit Ambitioso and Supervacuo.)
DUKE.
(To Lords.)
　Here's ambition with a poorly covering.
　I will prevent their envies; sure it was
　But some mistaken fury in our son
　Which these aspiring boys would climb upon;
　Release him suddenly.
NENCIO.
　　　　　　　My lord?
DUKE.
　　　　　　　　　We pardon him.
NENCIO.
　He owes your grace much thanks, and we much duty.
SORDIDO.
　We'll set release in motion presently.
DUKE.
　And call me hither one Piato, he
　That serves my son of late; I'll have some question
　With him.
SORDIDO.
　　　　With all good speed, my gracious lord.

(Exit Nencio and Sordido.)
DUKE.

> It well becomes that judge to nod at crimes
> That does commit greater himself and lives.
> I may forgive a disobedient error
> That expect pardon for adultery,
> And in my old days am a youth in lust.
> Many a beauty have I turned to poison
> In the denial, covetous of all.

(Music.)

> The heat within doth rise alike the sun
> Yet sets it ne'er till sunk in virgin dung.
> Piato, my son's servant, is a bawd,
> I'm told. Well, now he shall procure for me.
> Age hot is like a monster to be seen:
> My hairs are white and yet my sins are green.

(Exeunt.)

Scene 8

The street. Ambitioso and Supervacuo.

SUPERVACUO.

> Brother, let my opinion sway you once;
> I speak it for the best to have him die —
> If the signet come unto the judges' hands
> Why then his doom will be deferred till trials.

AMBITIOSO.

> In troth tis true.

SUPERVACUO.

>   Then let us pass the judges
> And fall to th'officers; tis but mistaking
> The Duke our father's meaning; where he named
> 'Ere many days' tis but forgetting that
> And have him die i'th'morning.

AMBITIOSO.

>   Excellent!

Then am I heir — Duke in a minute!

SUPERVACUO.

(Aside.)

                            Nay,
An' he were once puffed out, here is a pin
Should quickly prick your bladder.

AMBITIOSO.

                          Blest occasion!
Lussurioso packed, we'll have some trick
To wind our younger brother out of prison
That lies in for the rape; the lady's dead
And people's thoughts will soon be burièd.

SUPERVACUO.

We may with safety do't and live and feed:
The Duchess' sons are far too proud to bleed.

AMBITIOSO.

We are i'faith, too true. Come, let's not linger —
I'll to the officers, go you before
And set an edge upon the executioner.

SUPERVACUO.

Let me alone to grind him.

(Exit.)

AMBITIOSO.

                        Meet, farewell.

(Music.)

I am next now, I rise just in that place
Where thou'rt cut off — upon thy neck stepbrother;

(Enter Lussurioso.)

The falling of one head lifts up another.

(Exeunt.)

Scene 9

Jail cell. Lussurioso with Nencio, Sordido, First and Second Officers releasing him.

LUSSURIOSO.
  My lords, I am indebted to your loves
  For this, O this delivery.
NENCIO.
                But our duties
  My lord unto the hopes that grow in you.
LUSSURIOSO.
  If e'er I live to be the Duke, I'll thank you.
(Exeunt.)

Scene 10

Street near jail. Enter Ambitioso and Supervacuo to First Officer.

AMBITIOSO.
  Officer! Here's the Duke's signet; this warrant
  Brings the command of present death with it
  Unto our brother the Duke's son. We're sorry
  That we are so unnaturally employed
  In such an unkind office.
SUPERVACUO.
                But you know
  The Duke's command must be obeyed. Alas.
FIRST OFFICER.
  It must and shall my lord — this morning then,
  So suddenly?
AMBITIOSO.
          Ay alas poor good soul.

SUPERVACUO.
The Duke's behest is execution quick.
FIRST OFFICER.
My office shall be swift.
AMBITIOSO.

Therein you show
Yourself a good and upright officer.
Pray let him die as private as you may;
Do us that favor, spare him public shame.
Will you be so far kind?
FIRST OFFICER.

None shall witness it.
AMBITIOSO.
Why we do thank you; if we live to be
What we should be — that is the Duke myself —
You shall have a better office.
FIRST OFFICER.

Your lordship.
SUPERVACUO.
Commend us to the scaffold in our tears.
FIRST OFFICER.
I'll weep for you, and pray for your promotion.
(Exit.)
AMBITIOSO.
Fine fools in office!
SUPERVACUO.

Things fall out so fit!
AMBITIOSO.
So happily! Come, brother, ere next clock
His head will stand upon a bigger block.
(Exeunt.)

Scene 11

The bowels of the palace. A curtained archway. Vindice, disguised as Piato, is drawing the curtain shut as Hippolito enters.

VINDICE.
O sweet, delectable, rare, happy ravishing!
HIPPOLITO.
Why, what's the matter brother?
VINDICE.

         O tis able
To make a man spring up and knock his head
Against yon silver ceiling.
HIPPOLITO.

        Prithee tell me
Why may I not partake with you? Once you vowed
To give me share to every tragic thought.
VINDICE.
I think I did too.
Then I'll divide it to thee. The old Duke,
Thinking my outward shape and inward heart
Are cut out of one piece — hires me to greet
Him with a lady in some darkened place
Veiled from th'eyes o'th'court, to which I easily
Consented, and did wish his impudent grace
To meet her here, wherein tis night at noon;
And more, unto the torturing of his soul
The bastard and the Duchess have appointed
A meeting too in this luxurious circle —
Which most afflicting sight will kill his eyes
Before we kill the rest of him.
HIPPOLITO.
Twill i'faith, most dreadfully digested.
I see not how you could have missed me, brother.
VINDICE.
True, but the violence of my joy forgot it.

HIPPOLITO.

Ay. But where's that lady now?

VINDICE.

O at that word

I'm in a throng of happy apprehensions!

You shall be witness, brother,

Be ready, stand with your hat off.

(Goes behind curtain.)

HIPPOLITO.

Troth, I wonder what lady it should be.

(Vindice draws curtain, walking out a dress form on wheels, fully dressed, with Gloriana's skull attached as the head, veiled and masked.)

VINDICE.

Madam, his grace will not be absent long.

Silver? Ne'er doubt us, madam. Twill be worth

Three silken gowns unto your ladyship.

Disgrace? No hiding in that poor thin shell:

Tis the best grace you have to do it well;

I'll save your hand that labor, I'll unmask you.

(Removes mask.)

HIPPOLITO.

Why brother, brother.

VINDICE.

Art thou beguiled now?

Have I not fitted the old careless lecher

With a quaint piece of beauty?

HIPPOLITO.

This is she

Once was the lady stood betrothed to thee!

VINDICE.

The very same. And now methinks I could

E'en chide myself for doting on her beauty.

Does the silkworm expend her yellow labors

For thee? For thee does she undo herself?

Does every proud and self-affecting dame

Camphor her face for this, and grieve her maker

In sinful baths of milk while infants starve,

For her superfluous outside? — Lordships sold

To maintain ladyships for the poor benefit

Of a bewitching minute? — All for this?

Surely we're all mad people, and they

Whom we think are, are not: we mistake those;
Tis we are mad in sense, they but in clothes.
HIPPOLITO.

Faith and in clothes too, we give us our due.
VINDICE.

Who now bids twenty crown a night, prepares
Music, perfumes and banquets? All are hushed;
Thou may'st lie chaste now. It were fine methinks
T'have thee seen at revels, forgetful feasts
And unclean brothels; sure twould fright the sinner
And make him turn puritan, put a reveler
Out of his antic amble to philosopher
And cloy an epicure with empty dishes.
Here might a woman, scornful and ambitious,
Look through and through herself. See, ladies, with false forms
You deceive men but cannot deceive worms.
Now to my tragic business. Look you, brother,
I have not fashioned this only for show
And useless property, no — it shall bear a part
E'en in its own revenge. This very skull,
Whose mistress the Duke poisoned with this drug,
(Pulls out poison.)
The mortal curse o'th'earth, shall be revenged
In the like strain and kiss his lips to death.
(Applies poison to skull.)
As much as the old man can, he shall feel;
What fails in poison we'll supply in steel.
HIPPOLITO.

Brother, I do applaud thy constant vengeance,
The sharpness of thy malice, above thought.
VINDICE.

So tis laid on: Now come and welcome, Duke,
I have her for thee.
DUKE.
(Off.)
Piato!
HIPPOLITO.

      Hark, the Duke's come.
VINDICE.

                        Peace — Brother,
Fall you back a little with the bony lady.

HIPPOLITO.

That I will.

(Takes her behind curtain.)

VINDICE.

So, so —

Now nine years' vengeance crowd into a minute.

(Enter the Duke.)

Your good grace.

DUKE.

Piato! Hast brought her? What lady ist?

VINDICE.

Faith, my lord, a country lady, a little bashful at first as most of
them are, but after the first kiss, my lord, the worst is past with
them. She's somewhat a grave look with her, but —

DUKE.

I love that best, conduct her.

VINDICE.

Have at all.

(Goes to curtain.)

DUKE.

In gravest looks the greatest faults seem less:

Give me that sin that's robed in holiness.

(Vindice opens curtain and Hippolito walks out the dress form.)

Lady, sweetly encountered:

I came from court.

I must be bold with you —

(Kisses the skull.)

O! What's this? O!

VINDICE.

Royal villain, white devil!

DUKE.

O!

VINDICE.

Look closely now with thine affrighted eyeballs

And stare into these hollows. Duke, dost know

This dreadful mask? View it well; tis the skull

Of Gloriana, whom thou poisondst last.

DUKE.

O t'as poisoned me!

VINDICE.

Didst not know that till now?

DUKE.
What are you two?

(Hippolito steps out.)

VINDICE.

Villains, all three! The very ragged bone
Has been sufficiently revenged.

HIPPOLITO.
My lord,

What service may I perform?

DUKE.
O Hippolito —

Call treason!

HIPPOLITO.
Yes, my good lord. Treason, treason, treason!

(Stamping on him.)

DUKE.

Then I'm betrayed.

VINDICE.
Alas poor lecher.

DUKE.

My teeth are eaten out.

VINDICE.
Hadst any left?

HIPPOLITO.

I think but few.

VINDICE.
Then those that once did eat are eaten.

DUKE.

O my tongue!

VINDICE.

Your tongue? Old fool, twill teach you to kiss closer,
Not like a slobbering Frenchman. You have eyes still:
Look, monster, what a lady hast thou made me
My once-betrothèd wife.

(Removes skull.)

DUKE.
Is it thou villain?

Nay then —

VINDICE.
Tis I, tis Vindice, tis I!

68

HIPPOLITO.
>And let this comfort thee: our lord and father
>Fell sick upon th'infection of thy frowns
>And died in sadness; be that thy hope of life.

DUKE.
>   O!

VINDICE.
>He had his tongue, yet grief made him die speechless.
>Puh, tis but early yet; now I'll begin
>To stick thy soul with ulcers: Mark me, Duke,
>Thou'rt a renownèd, high, and mighty cuckold!

DUKE.
>O!

VINDICE.
>   Thy bastard with thy Duchess rides
>A-hunting in thy brow.

DUKE.
>   Millions of deaths!

VINDICE.
>Here in this spot they meet for damnèd clips:
>Those eyes shall see the incest of their lips.

DUKE.
>O villains!

(Opera from off: Otello.)

HIPPOLITO.
>   Hark, music!

VINDICE.
>   They're coming now.

DUKE.
>O kill me not with that sight.

VINDICE.
>Thou shalt not lose that sight for all thy Dukedom.

DUKE.
>Traitors, murderers!

VINDICE.
>   What, is not thy tongue eaten out yet?
>Then we'll invent a silence.

DUKE.
>   Treason! Murder!

VINDICE.
>Nay, faith, we'll have you hushed.

(To Hippolito:)

Now with thy dagger,
Nail down his tongue, and mine shall keep possession
About his heart; if he but gasp he dies.
Brother, if he but wink to 'void the sight,
Let our two other hands tear up his lids
And make his eyes, like comets, shine through blood.
(Hippolito stabs the Duke's tongue to the floor.)
When the bad bleeds, then is the tragedy good.
HIPPOLITO.
Whist, brother, music's at our ear: they come.
(Enter Spurio the bastard and the Duchess, they kiss.)
SPURIO.
Had not that kiss a taste of sin twere sweet.
DUCHESS.
Why, there's no pleasure sweet but it is sinful.
SPURIO.
True, such a bitter sweetness fate hath given;
Best side to us, is the worst side to heaven.
DUCHESS.
Push, come, tis the old Duke thy doubtful father —
The thought of him rubs heaven in thy way.
SPURIO.
Why tis a thought which ne'er had life.
So deadly do I loathe him for my birth
That if he took me hasped within his bed,
I would add murder to adultery.
(Music louder.)
DUCHESS.
Why, now thou'rt sociable: Let's in and feast.
Loud music sounds: pleasure is banquet's guest.
(Exit Spurio and Duchess.)
DUKE.
I cannot brook —
VINDICE.
The brook is turned to blood.
(Vindice and Hippolito put out the Duke's eyes and Vindice stabs him to death. To skull:)
Thou mayst rest now sweet, art not pleased?
Thou art revenged.

HIPPOLITO.
   Thanks to loud music.
VINDICE.
                              Twas our friend indeed;
   Tis state, in music for a Duke to bleed.
   Now but remains for us to seek a tune
   To play upon his son, and jangle soon:
   The Dukedom wants a head, though yet unfound;
   As fast as they peep up, let's cut 'em down!
(Music: Verdi's Otello, *final phrase of Act Two, "Dio vendicator!"*
Vindice and Hippolito, covered in blood, close the curtain.)

End of Act One

ACT TWO

Scene 1

The street. Enter the Duchess' two sons Ambitioso and Supervacuo, celebrating.

AMBITIOSO.
    Was not Lussurioso's execution
    Rarely plotted? Now we are the Duke's sons.
SUPERVACUO.
    Ay, you may thank my policy for that.
AMBITIOSO.
    Your policy for what?
SUPERVACUO.
                       Why, wast not my
    Invention t'slip the judges, and to draw
    The model of his death through sudden officer?
AMBITIOSO.
    Heart twas a thing I thought on too.
SUPERVACUO.
    You thought on't too! Sfoot, slander not your thoughts
    With glorious untruth, I know twas from you.
AMBITIOSO.
    I say twas in my head.
SUPERVACUO.
                    Like your brains then:
    Ne'er to come out as long as you do live.
AMBITIOSO.
    You'd have the honor on't forsooth that your wit
    Led him to th'scaffold?
SUPERVACUO.
               Since it is my due
    I'll publish't — but I'll ha't, in spite of you.

AMBITIOSO.

Methinks y'are much too bold, you should a little
Remember us brother, next to be honest Duke.

SUPERVACUO.

Ay, it shall be as easy for you to be Duke
As to be honest, and that's never.

AMBITIOSO.

                                 Sayst thou?

SUPERVACUO.

I say thou hast not brains for that high office.

AMBITIOSO.

For saying so, thy brains shall out thine head
When I am Duke.

SUPERVACUO.

                      Nay, do not wait till then —
Let's have it now!

AMBITIOSO.

                    I'll take thee at thy word then!

(Wrestle.)

O to have a brother so sickly vain —

SUPERVACUO.

Worse: to be brothered to one with moist brain!

AMBITIOSO.

O the curse: a brother of no more worth
Than extra digits on my hand, superfluous!

SUPERVACUO.

Admit the trick was mine.

AMBITIOSO.

                       Lussurios'

We both conveyed!

SUPERVACUO.

                   And there we both do joy!

AMBITIOSO.

Well, cold he is by this time, and because
We're both ambitious be't our amity,
And let the glory be shared equally.

SUPERVACUO.

I am content to that.

AMBITIOSO.

                Why then content.

(Releases.)

This night our younger brother shall be free:
I have a trick.
SUPERVACUO.
        A trick? What ist?
AMBITIOSO.
               We'll get
Him out of prison by a wile.
SUPERVACUO.
               What wile?
AMBITIOSO.
No sir, you shall not know't till it be done,
For then you'd swear twere yours.
(Enter First Officer with a bleeding head in a blood-soaked bag.)
             Here comes the officer.
SUPERVACUO.
Desired news.
AMBITIOSO.
       How now, my friend?
FIRST OFFICER.
                I'm allotted
To that desertless office to present you
With the yet bleeding head —
AMBITIOSO.
(Aside.)
          Tis well.
SUPERVACUO.
(Aside.)
              Ha, excellent!
AMBITIOSO.
(Aside.)
All's sure our own — Brother, canst weep, thinkst thou?
SUPERVACUO.
(Aside.)
For him I hate?
AMBITIOSO.
(Aside.)
        I'll teach thee to dissemble:
Good officer, our sorrows are so fluent
Our eyes o'erflow our tongues; words spoke in tears
Are like the murmurs of waters, the sound
Is loudly heard but cannot be distinguished.

SUPERVACUO.
   How died he, pray?
FIRST OFFICER.
                    O full of rage and spleen.
AMBITIOSO.
   He died most valiantly then: troth, we're glad
   To hear't.
FIRST OFFICER.
            I could not woo him once to pray.
SUPERVACUO.
   He showed himself a gentleman in that,
   Give him his due.
FIRST OFFICER.
               But in the stead of prayer
   He drew forth oaths.
AMBITIOSO.
                Then did he pray, dear heart,
   Although you understood him not.
FIRST OFFICER.
                    My lords,
   E'en at his last — with pardon be it spoke —
   He cursed you both.
SUPERVACUO.
               He cursed us? 'Las good soul.
AMBITIOSO.
   It was not in our powers, but the Duke's pleasure.
(Aside:)
   Finely dissembled on both sides! Sweet fate!
SUPERVACUO.
   Now for the head —
(Enter Lussurioso with Nencio and Sordido.)
LUSSURIOSO.
            Now my lords, well met —
AMBITIOSO and SUPERVACUO.
                            O!
LUSSURIOSO.
   Why d'you shun me, brothers? You may come nearer now,
   The savor of the prison has forsook me,
   I thank such kind lords as yourselves I'm free.
SUPERVACUO.
   — Alive!

AMBITIOSO.

      In health!

SUPERVACUO.

            Released! —

AMBITIOSO.

We were both e'en amazed with joy to see it.

LUSSURIOSO.

I am much to thank you.

AMBITIOSO.

                — Faith,

We spared no tongue unto my lord the Duke.

SUPERVACUO.

I know your delivery

Had not been half so sudden but for us.

AMBITIOSO.

O how we pleaded.

LUSSURIOSO.

         Most deserving brothers;

In my best studies I will think of it.

(Exit Lussurioso, Nencio, Sordido.)

AMBITIOSO.

O death and vengeance!

SUPERVACUO.

         Hell and torments!

AMBITIOSO.

                 Slave!

Cam'st thou to delude us?

FIRST OFFICER.

        Delude you, lords?

SUPERVACUO.

Ay villain —

AMBITIOSO

     Where's this head now?

FIRST OFFICER.

           Why, here my lord.

You brought me warrant to behead your brother.

SUPERVACUO.

Ay, our brother, the Duke's son.

FIRST OFFICER.

      The Duke's son,

My lord, had his release before you came.

AMBITIOSO.
    Whose head's that, then?
FIRST OFFICER.
                                    His, whom you left command for —
    Your own brothers.
(Offers bag.)
AMBITIOSO.
                            Our brothers? — O furies!
(Takes bag.)
SUPERVACUO.
    Plagues!
AMBITIOSO.
                    Confusions!
SUPERVACUO.
                                Darkness!
AMBITIOSO.
                                        Devils!
    Fell it so accursedly?
SUPERVACUO.
                            So damnedly?
AMBITIOSO.
    Villain, I'll brain thee with it!
(Swings bag.)
FIRST OFFICER.
                            O my lord!
AMBITIOSO.
    The devil overtake thee!
(Exit Officer running.)
SUPERVACUO.
                            — O fatal!
(Drops bag.)
AMBITIOSO.
    Prodigious to our bloods!
SUPERVACUO.
                            Did we dissemble?
AMBITIOSO.
    Did we make our tears women for thee?
(Hands in bag.)
SUPERVACUO.
    Bring warrant for thy death?

AMBITIOSO.

Mock off thy head? —

(Both look in bag.)
SUPERVACUO.

You had a trick, you had a wile forsooth.
AMBITIOSO.

A plague o'wiles! A plague o'tricks! I see now
There is nothing sure in mortality
But mortality. Well, no more words.
Dear brother, thou shalt be revenged by us.
Come, throw off clouds now, brother; think of vengeance
And deeper settled hate. Lussurioso,
Stepbrother, this act is thine; now sit fast:
Though we pull down all, thou shalt down at last!
(Opera: Otello, "Dio vendicator!" The brothers exit, daggers drawn and bag in hand.)

Scene 2

Lussurioso's chambers. Hippolito and Lussurioso.

LUSSURIOSO.
    Hippolito.
HIPPOLITO.
            My lord.
LUSSURIOSO.
                Be nearer, draw nearer;
    You're not so good methinks, I'm angry with you.
HIPPOLITO.
    With me, my lord? I'm angry with myself for't.
LUSSURIOSO.
    You did prefer a goodly fellow to me:
    Twas wittily elected, twas — I thought
    He'd been a villain, and he proves a knave;
    To me a knave!
HIPPOLITO.
    Tis much my sorrow if neglect in him

Breed discontent in you.

LUSSURIOSO.

Neglect? Twas will:
Firmly to tell of an abhorrent act
Twixt my stepmother and the bastard — O,
Incestuous sheets between 'em!

HIPPOLITO.

Fie, my lord.

LUSSURIOSO.

I, full of fury loyal to my father,
Committed treason on the lawful bed
For which I was within a stroke of death.

HIPPOLITO.

Alack, I'm sorry.

LUSSURIOSO.

Has greatly moved me!
But I'll recover to the ruin of that slave.
Twas told me lately that you have a brother.

HIPPOLITO.

Who, I? Yes my good lord, I have a brother.

LUSSURIOSO.

How chance the court ne'er saw him? How does he
Apply his hours?

HIPPOLITO.

Good faith, in cursing fate
Who, as he thinks, ordained him to be poor;
Keeps at home full of want and discontent.

LUSSURIOSO.

I have a service then I think him fit for;
Hippolito, repair him to us.

HIPPOLITO.

My lord, he will attend your pleasure straight;
But he's a man in whom much melancholy dwells.

LUSSURIOSO.

Why, the better: bring him to me at once.

HIPPOLITO.

With willingness and speed.

(Aside:)

Whom he disdained in scoff
E'en now, must now succeed. Brother, disguise must off!

(Exit.)

LUSSURIOSO.
This fellow will come fitly; he shall kill
That slave Piato: I'll employ thee, brother;
Slaves are but nails to drive out one another.
(Enter Nencio and Sordido.)
SORDIDO and NENCIO.
Good day unto your honor!
LUSSURIOSO.
And to you.
SORDIDO.
Saw you my lord the duke?
LUSSURIOSO.
Why, is he from the court?
NENCIO.
He's sure from court,
But where, we know not, neither can we hear on't.
LUSSURIOSO.
O he's rode forth.
NENCIO.
Twas wondrous privately.
SORDIDO.
There's none i'th'court had any knowledge on't.
LUSSURIOSO.
His grace is old, and sudden; what in us
Would appear vain, in him seems virtuous.
NENCIO.
Tis oracle, my lord.
(Exeunt.)

Scene 3

Antonio's apartment. Antonio and Pietro.

PIETRO.
My lord, I beg of you!
ANTONIO.
Thou urgest that thou knowst I cannot do.

PIETRO.
> Honorable Antonio, the respect you have
> For law, I have as much, nay more, for you;
> Have I not ever been in friendship loyal
> And e'en now plead but your behalf? When now
> Discordant strings are plucked, tis time to strike.
> The court's corruption can no lower sink;
> They revel, intrigue, while our purposed dreams
> Of honor and integrity through law
> Rot beneath the weighted stench of lies.
> No fitter time than now t'enforce a change,
> No man more fit to rule than you. Need
> You more example than your wife's disgrace
> At the dirty hands of power and how
> The crime is now forgot, ere justice lift
> Her scales, shameless, as it had never been?
> This does demand revenge.

ANTONIO.
>   Yet ghosts demand
> I will not stoop unto that act.

PIETRO.
>   Then who
> Will lead the righteous few to rise and cleanse
> Our sullied streets, which have grown dark and wet
> With sin? From court a rancid rain descends
> To pools of pitch; lust and liberty
> Creep in the minds and marrows of our youth
> And 'gainst the stream of virtue they now strive.

ANTONIO.
> Hast seen, O sun, in all thy journey, lechery
> Such as swells the bladder of our court?

PIETRO.
> All have forgot all good.

ANTONIO.
>   — And yet
> To take the law from evil, even good
> Ought not break it; I'll not usurper turn.

PIETRO.
> Must we then sit a freezing audience
> Upon our hands? Watch in dumb idleness
> While smug they trample all morality?

ANTONIO.
Though this city, yea, the whole country be corrupt,
My heart is armored and my soul all armed
With weapons of the law — for God on high
Doth fight 'longside the truth, and cannot fall.

PIETRO.
Pray't be so. Yet times hath been when God
Didst call an earthly hand to act his will.

ANTONIO.
Such a call did ne'er resound so shrill.

PIETRO.
Prithee think upon't.

(Exit.)

ANTONIO.
                              Ay, ay.
My wife's bestainèd corpse doth cry for vengeance!
The cursèd sleep of suicide will ne'er
Be restful till a peace is made for her —
Yet tis forbidden by both God and law.
This emptiness doth at my entrails claw.
Down, down! O God, give me the strength to quench
The fires of lust and vengeance that do burn
This mortal breast. O! To purge my love,
I must have flesh. God spare my soul above.

(Exeunt.)

Scene 4

Lussurioso's chamber. Enter Vindice as himself and Hippolito.

HIPPOLITO.
He that did lately in disguise reject thee
Shall, now thou art thyself, as much respect thee.

VINDICE.
Well, I must suit myself to his desires
What color-so-e'er they be, hoping next
To thrust up all my wishes in his breast.

HIPPOLITO.
    You fetch 'bout well; but let's talk in present.
    You must change tongue — familiar was your first.
VINDICE.
    I'll bear me in some strain of melancholy,
    String myself with heavy-sounding wire
    And pluck it darkly.
HIPPOLITO.
               Why tis as I meant,
    I gave you out at first in discontent.
(Enter Lussurioso.)
    Sfoot, here he comes — Hast thought upon't?
VINDICE.

                            Salute him,
    Fear not me.
(Creates a new disguise.)
LUSSURIOSO.
           Hippolito.
HIPPOLITO.
              My lord.
LUSSURIOSO.
                  What's he yonder?
HIPPOLITO.
    Tis Vindice, my discontented brother.
LUSSURIOSO.
    Come nearer.
HIPPOLITO.
             Brother: lord Lussurioso,
    The Duke's son.
LUSSURIOSO.
           Be more near to us.
VINDICE.
                 How don you?
    God you god 'en.
LUSSURIOSO.
             — Be nearer still.
VINDICE.
    Troth la, I beg your mercy, my humour makes me loathe all
      ceremony.
LUSSURIOSO.
    Tell me, what doth discontent thee?

VINDICE.

That I can find no perfume yet to sweeten out duplicity.

LUSSURIOSO.

Where hast thou smelt it most?

VINDICE.

Most? In this descent, la — politicians, mothers, and virgins. The first tis common and expected; the second, as rampant as the first, but commonly unexpected. Yet worst of all in virgin maids.

LUSSURIOSO.

Why there worst of all?

VINDICE.

Purity ist temptation, therefore duplicity exemplified. A sniff of chastity has many a full stomach turned. And those that eat of it, I disgust to name 'em: riotous whore-hounds clothed in silk, their shameless faces masked in silver burnished titles.

LUSSURIOSO.

And all this makes thee a man melancholy?

VINDICE.

Tis food to some, my lord. In me it roils and thunders till I vomit up the thought of such a dame in bloody bile and pray to skewer the flesh of that beasty man, roast it o'er the flames of honor as a great revenger's feast.

LUSSURIOSO.

You name but easy pleasures with no harm in 'em.

VINDICE.

Ay, ay, no harm, lord sir, la, a trifle is the maiden fallen from grace, grace herself turned bawd. But this is the meat of my melancholy; mark it: a streaming pestilence of hypocrisy that poisons the body of the state and plagues the people in it; lies are dipped in honeyed words and 'slud you what more worse? the people eat th'lies for truth, sith it goes simply down and out. All the world's a brothel's pit to me; the men are drunk lecherous claps and the women — 'slud, the women are rotting whores o'mutton.

LUSSURIOSO.

I'faith, thou hast a parlous melancholy!

I think thou art ill-moneyed?

VINDICE.

Money! Puh!

T'as been my want so long tis now my scoff;

I've e'en forgot what color silver's of.

84

LUSSURIOSO.
(Giving Vindice silver coin.)
    Somewhat to set thee up withal.
VINDICE.

                  O my lord!

LUSSURIOSO.
    You shall be better yet if you but fasten
    Truly on my intent. Now y'are both present
    I will unbrace a villain to your vengeful blades,
    Who hath disgraced you much and injured us.
HIPPOLITO.
    Disgraced us, my lord?
LUSSURIOSO.

                Ay, Hippolito:
    I kept it here till now that both your angers
    Might meet him at once.
VINDICE.

               I am covetous
    To know the villain.
LUSSURIOSO.
(To Hippolito.)

             You know him — that slave Piato
    Led me e'en to raze my father's bosom.
VINDICE.
(Aside.)
    All this is I!
HIPPOLITO.
        Ist he, my lord?
LUSSURIOSO.

              I'll tell you —
    You first preferred him to me.
VINDICE.

           Did you, brother?
HIPPOLITO.
    I did indeed.
LUSSURIOSO.
        And the ungrateful villain
    To quit that kindness, strongly wrought with me
    For jewels with to corrupt your virgin sister.

HIPPOLITO.
  O villain!
VINDICE.
            He shall surely die that did it.
LUSSURIOSO.
  I, far from thinking any virgin harm,
  Especially knowing her to be too chaste
  To touch, would not endure him —
VINDICE.
                        Would you not
  My lord? Twas wondrous honorably done.
LUSSURIOSO.
  But with some fine frowns kept him out.
VINDICE.
                  Out slave!
LUSSURIOSO.
  What did me he, but in revenge of that
  Went of his own free will to make infirm
  Your sister's honor (whom I honor with my soul
  For chaste respect) and, not prevailing there —
  In mere spleen, by the way — waylays your mother,
  Whose honor (being a coward as it seems)
  Yielded by little force.
VINDICE.
              Coward indeed.
HIPPOLITO.
  Did she succumb to him?
LUSSURIOSO.
              She was much willing.
HIPPOLITO.
(To Vindice.)
  Was she so?
VINDICE.
          Ay, so, she'll burn for't. Th'event!
LUSSURIOSO.
  He, proud of this advantage, as he thought,
  Brought me these news for happy; but I —
  Heaven forgive me for't —
VINDICE.
            What did your honor?

LUSSURIOSO.

In rage I pushed him from me to the floor,
Trampled beneath his throat, spurned him and bruised;
Indeed I was too cruel, to say the truth.

HIPPOLITO.

Most nobly done.

VINDICE.

(Aside.)

                    Has not heaven an ear?
Is all the lightning wasted?

LUSSURIOSO.

If I were so impatient in a modest cause,
What should you be?

VINDICE.

                    Full mad: he shall not live
To see the moon change.

LUSSURIOSO.

                    Yet for my hate's sake,
Hippolito entice him here and suddenly.

HIPPOLITO.

I'll go seek him.

(Aside:)

                What now, brother?

VINDICE.

(Aside.)

Nay, e'en what you will; y'are put to't, brother!

HIPPOLITO.

(Aside.)

An impossible task I'll swear,
To bring him hither that's already here.

(Exit.)

LUSSURIOSO.

Thy name? I have forgot it.

VINDICE.

                    Vindice.

LUSSURIOSO.

Tis a good name, that.

VINDICE.

                Ay — a revenger.

LUSSURIOSO.

It does betoken courage; thou shouldst valiant be

And kill thine enemies.

VINDICE.

That's my hope, my lord.

LUSSURIOSO.

This slave is one.

VINDICE.

I'll doom him.

LUSSURIOSO.

Then I'll praise thee.
Do thou observe me best and I'll best raise thee.

(Reenter Hippolito.)

VINDICE.

Indeed I thank you.

LUSSURIOSO.

Now Hippolito,
Where's that slave?

HIPPOLITO.

Not in state now to be seen;
The worst of all the deadly sins is in him,
That beggarly damnation: drunkenness.

LUSSURIOSO.

Then he's a double slave. What, are you both
Firmly resolved? I'll see him dead myself!

VINDICE.

Or else let me not live.

HIPPOLITO.

We shall do all.

LUSSURIOSO.

Rise but in this and you shall never fall.

HIPPOLITO.

Your Honor's vassals.

(Exit Lussurioso.)

VINDICE.

O thou almighty patience, tis my wonder
That such a fellow, impudent and wicked,
Should not be cloven as he stood
Or with a secret wind burst open!
Is there no thunder left, or ist kept up
In stock for heavier vengeance?

(Thunder.)

There it goes!

(They laugh. Thunder again.)
HIPPOLITO.

Brother, we lose ourselves.
VINDICE.

But I have found it!

HIPPOLITO.

What ist?
VINDICE.

Tis sound and good, thou shalt partake it:
I'm hired to kill myself.
HIPPOLITO.

True.

VINDICE.

Prithee mark it;

And the old Duke is dead but not discovered.
HIPPOLITO.

Most true!
VINDICE.

What say you then to this device:

If we dressed up the body of the Duke —
HIPPOLITO.

As that Piato? Ha ha.
VINDICE.

Ha, y'are quick.

HIPPOLITO.

In that disguise of yours!
VINDICE.

Ha ha — y'ave reached it.

HIPPOLITO.

I like it wondrously.
VINDICE.

And 'being in drink,'

To lean him on his elbow as if sleeping —
Then call you hither that 'sir would-be Duke' —
HIPPOLITO.

Firmer and firmer.
VINDICE.

Doubt not, tis in grain.

HIPPOLITO.

Let's about it.

VINDICE.

But by the way, let's turn
Unto our mother —
HIPPOLITO.

Twas all true he said?
VINDICE.

Ay brother, to our shame.
HIPPOLITO.

A foul disgrace —
And would you keep this hid from me?
VINDICE.

Come, brother,
Let's purge that whoreson devil from our mother!
(Exeunt.)

Scene 5

A hallway in the palace. Enter the Duchess with the bastard Spurio; she seemeth lasciviously to him. Supervacuo and Ambitioso come upon them, hiding to observe.

SPURIO.
Madam, unlock yourself — should it be seen,
Your arm would be suspected libertine.
DUCHESS.
Who ist that dares suspect or this or these?
May not we deal our favors where we please?
SPURIO.
I'm confident you may.
(Exit Spurio and Duchess; after them Supervacuo runs with a blade.)
AMBITIOSO.

Sfoot brother, hold!
SUPERVACUO.
Wouldst let the bastard shame us?
AMBITIOSO.

Hold, hold brother!
There's fitter time than now.

SUPERVACUO.

                                   Now, when I see it!

AMBITIOSO.
    Tis too much seen already.

SUPERVACUO.

                             Seen and known:
    The nobler she grows, th'baser is she grown.

AMBITIOSO.
    If she were bent lasciviously — O death —
    Must she needs choose such an unequal sinner
    To make all worse?

SUPERVACUO.

                    A bastard!

AMBITIOSO.

                          Our disgrace!

SUPERVACUO.
    The Duke's bastard!

AMBITIOSO.

                  Shameless!

SUPERVACUO.

                     Shame heaped on shame!

AMBITIOSO.
    Come, stay not here: let's after and prevent
    Else they'll sin faster than we can repent.

(Exeunt.)

Scene 6

Gratiana's shop. Enter Vindice and Hippolito dragging out their mother Gratiana, daggers in their hands.

VINDICE.
    Wicked, unnatural parent!

HIPPOLITO.

                    Fiend of women!

GRATIANA.
    Mean my sons to murder me? Help!

VINDICE.

In vain.

GRATIANA.

Are you so barbarous, to set iron nipples
Upon the breast that gave you suck?

VINDICE.

That breast

Is turned to curdled poison.

GRATIANA.

Am not I your mother?

VINDICE.

Thou dost usurp that title now by fraud
For in that shell of mother breeds a bawd.

GRATIANA.

A bawd! Why tis a loathsome name, I hate it.

VINDICE.

Did not the Duke's son direct
A fellow of the world's condition hither
That did corrupt all that was good in thee,
And make thee work our sister to his lust?

GRATIANA.

That had been monstrous! I'd defy that man
Of any such intent.

VINDICE.

O I'm in doubt

Whether I'm myself or no — I was the man!
(Reveal.)

Defy me now. Let's see: do't modestly.

GRATIANA.

O hell unto my soul.

VINDICE.

In that disguise, I, sent from the Duke's son,
Tried you, and swayed you easily with base metal
As any villain might have done.

GRATIANA.

O no:

No tongue but yours could have bewitched me so.

VINDICE.

O nimble in damnation, quick in tune:
There is no devil could strike fire so soon!

HIPPOLITO.
A mother to give aim to her own daughter!
VINDICE.
True, brother: how far beyond nature tis,
Though many mothers do't!
GRATIANA.

O sons forgive —

(Weeps.)
VINDICE.
Nay and you draw tears once, put this to bed;
Wet will make iron blush and change to red:
Brother, it rains, twill spoil your dagger, house it.
HIPPOLITO.
Tis done.
(Sheathe daggers.)
GRATIANA.
You heavens, let these waters of mine eyes
Rinse this infectious spot out of my soul!
VINDICE.
Tis a sweet shower, it does much good.
O you of easy wax, how leprously
That office would have clinged unto your forehead.
All mothers that had any graceful hue
Would have worn masks to hide their face at you.
HIPPOLITO.
And then our sister full of hire and baseness —
VINDICE.
There turns my blood to boiling lead again!
She the Duke's son's great concubine,
A drab of state, a cloth-o'silver slut
To have her train borne up and let her soul
Trail i'th'dirt: great!
HIPPOLITO.
To be miserably great:
Rich, to be eternally wretched.
VINDICE.
A common whore!
GRATIANA.
O sons forgive me, to myself I'll prove more true;
You that should honor me — I kneel to you.
(Kneels.)

VINDICE.

Nay, I'll kiss you now; kiss her, brother.

(Kisses her.)

HIPPOLITO.

Let it be.

(Kisses her.)

VINDICE.

Let's marry her t'our souls, wherein's no lust,
And honorably love her.

HIPPOLITO.

                            Our business, brother.

VINDICE.

And well remembered: joy's a subtle elf,
I think man's happiest when he forgets himself.

GRATIANA.

I'll give you this: that one I never knew
Plead better for, and 'gainst the devil, than you.

VINDICE.

You make me proud on't.

GRATIANA.

You'll nevermore have cause to doubt my grace.

HIPPOLITO.

Commend us in all virtue to our sister.

VINDICE.

Ay, for the love of heaven, to that true maid.

GRATIANA.

With my best words.

VINDICE.

                        Why, that was motherly said.

(Exit Vindice and Hippolito.)

GRATIANA.

I wonder now that riches did transport me;
I feel good thoughts begin to settle in me;
I am myself again.

(Enter Castiza dressed as a prostitute.)

CASTIZA.

Now, mother, you have wrought with me so strongly
That for my advancement I am content —

GRATIANA.

Content to what?

CASTIZA.

                 To do as you have wished me,
To prostitute my breast to the Duke's son.

GRATIANA.

   I hope you will not so.

CASTIZA.

                    Hope you I will not?

GRATIANA.

   Truth but I do.

CASTIZA.

                  Do not deceive yourself:
I am, as you, e'en now a shameless thought.
What would you now, are ye not pleased yet with me?
You shall not wish me to be more lascivious
Than I intend to be.

GRATIANA.

                 Strike not me cold.

CASTIZA.

   How often have you charged me on your blessing
To be a cursèd woman! When you knew
Your blessing had no force to make me lewd
You laid your curse upon me. That did more —

GRATIANA.

   Good child, I am recovered of that foul disease —
Make me not sick in health. If then you say
My words prevailed when they were wickedness,
How much more now when they are just and good.

CASTIZA.

   Are you not she who taught me well the value
In our sex? the worth of every part?
And would you now untwist this red-hot serpent
You wound about me? Twas your hard persuasions
Won me. Are you not she that would so quickly
For such and such a sum, ravished be?

GRATIANA.

   Tis tedious to repeat what's past: I'm now
Your present mother.

CASTIZA.

               Push, now tis too late.

GRATIANA.

   Bethink again, thou knowst not what thou sayst.

CASTIZA.

No? — 'Deny advancement, treasure, the Duke's son?'

GRATIANA.

(Aside.)

O see, I spoke those words, and now they poison me!

(To Castiza.)

What will the deed do then?
Advancement? True, as high as shame can pitch;
For treasure? Who e'er knew a harlot rich?
The Duke's son! O when women are young courtiers
They are sure to be old beggars;
To know the miseries most harlots taste
Thou'd'st wish thyself unborn when thou'rt unchaste!

CASTIZA.

O mother, we are blest above our place —
A brief exchange of flesh and we with poor,
Shall untold riches suddenly have in store.

GRATIANA.

Such a man may lift thee for a moment;
So at his nipple mayst thou silver suck,
Yet that milkless breast so rich will curdle quick.
The next young maiden he doth spy shalt thrive
Whilst thy honor dies.

CASTIZA.

Mother, think me
Mongst thousand daughters happiest of all others:
Be I a glass for maids and thou for mothers.

(Exit.)

GRATIANA.

If this were a tragedy, methinks I should now
Cleave my stretched cheeks with sound, speak from all sense,
But loud and full of players' eloquence.
— No, no! What shall I eat?

(Exeunt.)

Scene 7

*The basement. Enter Vindice and Hippolito exhuming the
Duke's corpse. They dress him in Piato's cloak and arrange
him on steps as a sleeping drunk.*

VINDICE.
    So, so, he leans well; take heed you wake him not, brother.
HIPPOLITO.
    I warrant you, my life for yours.
VINDICE.
    That's a good bet, for I must kill myself! *(Points to corpse.)*
    Brother, that's I, that sits for me, do you mark it. And I must stand
    ready here to make away myself yonder; or myself must sit and
    stand to be killed — Ha! I could vary it ten times over —
HIPPOLITO.
    That's enough now, o'conscience.
VINDICE.

                                    Where is he now?

HIPPOLITO.
    Has been sent for.
LUSSURIOSO.
(Off.)

                        Hippolito!

VINDICE.

                                    Here he comes!

HIPPOLITO.
    My honored lord —
(Enter Lussurioso.)
LUSSURIOSO.

                        Now sirs, where is the villain?

HIPPOLITO.
    My lord, look — see there.
LUSSURIOSO.

                            Stay — yonder's the slave.

VINDICE.

There's the slave indeed, my lord.

(Aside to Hippolito:)

Tis a good child, he calls his father slave.

LUSSURIOSO.

Ay, that's the damnèd villain! Soft, tread easy.

VINDICE.

Puh, I warrant we'll stifle in our breaths.

LUSSURIOSO.

Base rogue, thou sleepst thy last! Be ready, nake

Your blades, think of your wrongs: this slave has injured you.

HIPPOLITO.

Troth, so he has —

VINDICE.

(Aside.) And he has paid well for't.

LUSSURIOSO.

Meet with him now.

VINDICE.

You'll bear us out, my lord?

LUSSURIOSO.

Puh, am I a lord for nothing, think you?

Quickly now!

VINDICE.

Sa, sa, sa —

(Stabs the corpse.)

HIPPOLITO.

— Thump!

VINDICE.

There he lies!

LUSSURIOSO.

Nimbly done.

(Approaches the corpse.)

What, stiff and cold already?

Ha! O villainy, tis the Duke my father!

— That villain Piato

Whom you thought now to kill has murdered him

And left him thus disguised.

HIPPOLITO.

Tis not unlikely.

LUSSURIOSO.

Tis his coat!

98

VINDICE.
>O rascal, was he not ashamed
To put the Duke into a greasy cloak?
LUSSURIOSO.
Has been dead and buried — who knows how long?
VINDICE.
(Aside.)
Marry that do I!
LUSSURIOSO.
>Ho, Nencio, Sordido!
No words, I pray, of anything intended.
HIPPOLITO.
Nought from us, my lord.
LUSSURIOSO.
>I'll forthwith send to court
For all the nobles, bastard, Duchess, all —
How here by accident we found him dead
And in his raiment; that foul villain fled!
VINDICE.
Twill be the best way, sir, to clear us all.
(Enter Nencio and Sordido.)
NENCIO and SORDIDO.
My lord —
SORDIDO.
>O what's the matter here?
LUSSURIOSO.
Choosing for private conference this sad spot
We found the Duke my father gealed in blood.
SORDIDO.
My lord the Duke! Run, hie thee Nencio,
Startle the court by signifying so much.
(Exit Nencio.)
LUSSURIOSO.
My royal father, too basely let blood
By a malevolent slave!
HIPPOLITO.
(Aside.)
>He calls thee slave!
VINDICE.
(Aside.)
Not I: Piato!

LUSSURIOSO.
                 O look! His lips are gnawn
   With poison!
VINDICE.
              His lips? By my life, they be!
LUSSURIOSO.
   O villain — O rogue — O slave —
AMBITIOSO.
(Off.)

                           Where?

SUPERVACUO.
(Off.)

                          Which way?
(Enter Ambitioso, Supervacuo, Duchess, Spurio and his Servant, Antonio, Pietro, Antonio's Lord, Nencio, and Officers.)
AMBITIOSO.
   Over what roof hangs this prodigious comet
   In deadly fire?
LUSSURIOSO.
            Behold, behold, my lords:
   The Duke my father's murdered by a vassal
   That wore this habit, and here left disguised.
DUCHESS.
   My lord and husband!
SUPERVACUO.
(Aside.)
   Learn of our mother — let's dissemble too!
   I'm glad he's vanquished: so I hope are you?
AMBITIOSO.
(Aside.)
   Ay, you may take my word for't.
SPURIO.
(Aside.)

                 Old Dad dead?
   I, one of his cast sins, will send the fates
   Most hearty commendations by his son.
HIPPOLITO.
(Aside.)
   How happy is our vengeance!

VINDICE.
(Aside.)

                                      Why it hits
Past apprehension of indifferent wits.
LUSSURIOSO.
Search posthaste to trap the villain.
(Officers exit.)
VINDICE.
(Aside.)

                                    Posthaste! Ha ha.
ANTONIO.
My lord, I'm something bold to speak your duty.
Your father's unexpectedly departed,
The titles that were due to him meet you.
LUSSURIOSO.
Meet me? I'm not at leisure, my good lord,
I've many griefs to dispatch out o'th'way.
(Officers pick up Duke.)
Lord Antonio —
ANTONIO.

                      The state will have a head.
NENCIO.
My lord, it is your shine must comfort us.
LUSSURIOSO.
Alas, I shine in tears like sun in April.
SORDIDO.
Let the sky turn May —
NENCIO.

                          You're now my lord's grace.
LUSSURIOSO.
My lord's grace? I perceive you'll have it so.
ANTONIO.
Tis but your own.
LUSSURIOSO.
Then heaven give me the grace to be so.
DUCHESS.
(To Antonio.)
Shalt he whose dagger wast at his father's breast
But two nights since now take's place on th'throne?
LUSSURIOSO.
Sure tis sudden grief that speaks.

(To Duchess.)

Be consoled:

The villain will be brought to law.

VINDICE.

No doubt

But time will make the murderer bring forth himself.

HIPPOLITO

(Aside.)

He were an ass then, i'faith!

NENCIO.

In the mean season

Let us bethink the latest funeral honors

Due to the Duke's cold body, and withal

(Officers remove Duke.)

Calling to memory our new happiness

Spread in his royal son — lords, gentlemen,

Prepare for revels!

PIETRO and VINDICE.

(Aside.)

Revels!

SORDIDO.

Time hath several falls:

Griefs lift up joys, feasts put down funerals.

ANTONIO.

Joy in moderation, reign in justice.

LUSSURIOSO.

All sorrows run their circles into joys.

(Exit Antonio, Pietro, Antonio's Lord.)

SORDIDO.

We'll crown my lord and then to revels! Come!

(Exit Lussurioso, Nencio and Sordido.)

HIPPOLITO.

(Aside.)

Revels.

VINDICE.

(Aside.)

Ay, that's the word! We are firm yet:

Strike one strain more and then we crown our wit.

(Exit Vindice and Hippolito.)

SPURIO.

(Aside to Duchess and Servant.)

Well, have at the fairest mark —
So said the Duke when he begot me.
In this masque we'll play a part.
And if I miss his heart, then flout
At any — a bastard scorns to be out.
(Exit Duchess, Spurio and Servant.)
SUPERVACUO.
   Not'st thou that Spurio, brother?
AMBITIOSO.

                              To our shame.
SUPERVACUO.
   His hair shall not grow longer. In these revels
   Tricks may be set afoot. Seest yon new moon?
   Twill outlive the new Duke by many days:
   This hand shall dispossess him: then we're mighty;
   Power's at our hands.
AMBITIOSO.

                   A revel's masque
   Is treason's license; that build upon —
   Tis murder's best face, when a mask is on!
(Exit.)
SUPERVACUO.
   And do you think to be Duke then, kind brother?
   I'll see fair play: drop one, and there lies t'other.
(Exeunt.)

Scene 8

*Pietro's quarters, Antonio's apartments. Enter Vindice and
Hippolito to Pietro and Antonio's Lord.*

VINDICE.
   My lords, strike old griefs into other countries
   That flow in too much milk and have faint livers,
   Not daring to stab home their discontents.
HIPPOLITO.
   Let our hid flames break out as fire, as lightning

To blast this villainous Dukedom vexed with sin.
PIETRO.
    How?
LORD.
          Which way?
HIPPOLITO.
                  Any way! Your wrongs are such,
We cannot justly be revenged too much.
VINDICE.
    You shall have all enough. Revels are toward,
    And those base nobles that have long suppressed you
    Are planning entertainments for th'new Duke;
    The Duchess' sons and Spurio the bastard
    Prepare the masque, and do themselves intend
    To dance afore Lussurioso's banquet.
HIPPOLITO.
    Sure they do mean some mischief too.
VINDICE.
                     No matter;
    The masquing suits are fashioning; now comes in
    The part which we must play: we to take pattern
    Of all those suits, the color, trimming, fashion,
    E'en to an undistinguished hair almost.
    Then entering first, and mimicking the form,
    Within a strain or two we shall find leisure
    To dance in step with darting swords in measure,
    And when they think their pleasure good and sweet,
    In midst of mirthful laughter they shall bleed!
PIETRO.
    Weightily, effectually!
LORD.
              Before
    The other masquers come —
HIPPOLITO.
                    We're gone, all done
    And past.
PIETRO.
          Revenge we shall enjoy at last.
    O good Hippolito —
VINDICE.
             Come my lords,

Prepare for deeds, let other times have words.
(Exeunt.)

Scene 9

Lussurioso's coronation. A grand red drape descends. Triumphant music. Enter Officers, Nencio, Sordido, Ambitioso, Supervacuo, Spurio, Duchess, Antonio. Enter Lussurioso, who is crowned by Antonio. Exeunt, except Nencio, Sordido, Lussurioso and Duchess. A banquet table covered in desserts and wine brought forth.

NENCIO.
(A toast.)
> Many harmonious hours and choicest pleasures
> Fill up the royal numbers of your years.

(They drink.)
LUSSURIOSO.
> My lord, we're pleased to thank you — though we know
> Tis but your duty now to wish it so.

NENCIO.
> That shine makes us all happy.

SORDIDO.
> His grace frowns.

NENCIO.
> Yet we must say he smiles.

SORDIDO.
> I think we must.

DUCHESS.
> My sons have promised us a pleasant spectacle.

LUSSURIOSO.
(Aside.)
> The Duchess is suspected foully bent;
> I'll begin Dukedom with her banishment.
> The bastard shall not live. After these revels
> I'll begin strange ones: He and the stepsons
> Shall pay their lives for th'first entertainments.

105

DUCHESS.
My gracious lord, please you prepare for pleasure;
The masque is not far off.
LUSSURIOSO.
We are for pleasure.
Take your places, lords.
(They sit at table facing the curtain. Music.)
SORDIDO.
I hear 'em coming, my lord.
(The grand drape rises to reveal a Danse Macabre in a large mirror: the masque of revengers [Vindice, Hippolito, Pietro, Antonio's Lord] all wearing red robes, white skull masks, and wielding swords.)
LUSSURIOSO.
Ah tis well —
(Aside:)
Brothers, and bastard, you dance next in hell!
(The revengers dance. At the end they steal out their swords and these four kill the four at the table. It thunders.)
VINDICE.
Thunder! Dost know thy cue?
HIPPOLITO.
So my lords, we have enough.
PIETRO.
Come away — no lingering!
HIPPOLITO.
Follow — go!
(Exit revengers, except Vindice.)
VINDICE.
No power is angry when the lustful die:
When thunder claps, God likes the tragedy.
(Exit.)
LUSSURIOSO.
O, O!
(The other masque of intended murderers [Ambitioso, Supervacuo, Spurio and Servant], dressed identically to the first group, enter dancing. Lussurioso recovers a little in voice and groans:)
A guard! Treason!
(At which they all start out of their measure, and they find them all to be murdered.)
SPURIO.
Whose groan was that?

LUSSURIOSO.

Treason. A guard.

SUPERVACUO.

— How now!

AMBITIOSO.

All murdered!

SPURIO.

Murdered!

SUPERVACUO.

The Duke!

SPURIO.

The Duchess!

AMBITIOSO and SUPERVACUO.

Our mother!

SERVANT.

And those his nobles!

AMBITIOSO.

(Aside.)

Here's a labor saved:
I thought to have sped him.

SPURIO.

Sblood — how came this?

AMBITIOSO.

Then I proclaim myself: Now I am Duke.

SUPERVACUO.

Thou Duke! Brother, thou liest.

(Supervacuo stabs Ambitioso.)

SPURIO.

Slave! So dost thou.

(Spurio stabs Supervacuo.)

SERVANT.

Base villain, hast thou slain the Duchess' sons?

(Servant stabs Spurio. Reenter the first men, Vindice, Hippolito, Pietro, and Antonio's Lord.)

VINDICE.

Treason, murder!

HIPPOLITO.

Help, guard!

VINDICE.

My lord the Duke!

(Enter Antonio and Officers.)

HIPPOLITO.
    Lay hold upon this traitor!
(Officers seize Servant.)
LUSSURIOSO.

                            O.

VINDICE.

                                    Alas

    The Duke is murdered.
HIPPOLITO.

                            And the brothers.

VINDICE.

                                            Surgeons, surgeons!

(Aside:)
    Heart, does he breathe so long?
ANTONIO.
    A piteous tragedy.
LUSSURIOSO.

                    Oh.

VINDICE.
(To Hippolito.)

                        Look to the Duke.

(To Servant:)
    Confess, thou murderous and unhallowed man,
    Didst thou kill all these?
SERVANT.

                            None but the bastard, I.

ANTONIO.
    How came the Duke slain then?
SERVANT.

                                We found him so.

LUSSURIOSO.
    O villain.
VINDICE.

            Hark.

LUSSURIOSO.

                    Those in the masque did murder us.

VINDICE.
    O marble impudence — will you confess now?
SERVANT.
    Sblood, tis all false!

ANTONIO.

                      Away with that foul monster
  Dipped in a prince's blood.
SERVANT.

                      Heart tis a lie!
ANTONIO.

  Let him have bitter execution.
(Exit Spurio's Servant guarded by Officer.)
VINDICE.

  See what confession doth.
HIPPOLITO.

  Who would not lie when men are hanged for truth?
VINDICE.

  How fares my lord the Duke?
LUSSURIOSO.

                  Farewell to all:
  He that climbs highest has the greatest fall.
  My tongue is out of office.
VINDICE.

                Air, gentlemen, air.
(Whispers:)
  Now thou'lt not prate on't, twas Vindice murdered thee!
LUSSURIOSO.

  O!
VINDICE.
(Whispers.)
      Murdered thy father!
LUSSURIOSO.

                   O!
VINDICE.
(Whispers.)

               And I am he!
(Slits his throat.)
  Tell nobody. —
(Lussurioso dies.)

          So, so. The Duke's departed.
ANTONIO.

  It was a deadly hand that wounded him;
  The rest, ambitious who should rule and sway
  Beyond his death, were so made all away.

HIPPOLITO.
My lord, tis likely.
VINDICE.

                       — Now the hope
O'th'city lies upon your reverence.
HIPPOLITO.
Your grace will make the golden age again,
When there was fewer, but more honest men.
ANTONIO.
The burden's weighty and will press me down:
May I so rule that heaven holds the crown.
PIETRO.
(Gives crown.)
The rape of your good lady has been 'quitted
With death on death.
ANTONIO.

                   Just is the law above.
But of all things it puts me most to wonder
How the old Duke came murdered.
VINDICE.

                        O my lord.
ANTONIO.
Twas strangely carried: I not heard the like.
He accused hath not been discovered.
HIPPOLITO.
Twas all done for the best, my lord.
VINDICE.

                       In troth,
An evil deed done for the general good.
ANTONIO.
How say you? Evil done for good?
VINDICE.

                       Ay, ay;
All for your graces' good. We may be bold
To speak it now: twas somewhat wittily carried
Though we say it. Twas we two murdered him!
HIPPOLITO.
Brother!
ANTONIO.
      You two?

VINDICE.

None else, i'faith my lord.

Nay, twas well managed.

ANTONIO.

Lay hands upon these villains.

VINDICE.

How? On us?

ANTONIO.

Bear 'em to speedy execution.

VINDICE.

Heart, wast not for your good, my lord?

HIPPOLITO.

Ay, for your good —

ANTONIO.

My good!

Away with 'em. Such a royal man as he?

You that would murder him would murder me!

VINDICE.

Ist come about?

HIPPOLITO.

You have us both undone.

VINDICE.

May not we set as well as the Duke's son?

Thou hast no conscience: are we not revenged?

Is there one enemy left alive 'mongst those?

Tis time to die when we ourselves are foes.

PIETRO.

When murderers shut deeds close, this curse does seal 'em:

If none disclose 'em, they themselves reveal 'em.

HIPPOLITO.

(To Vindice.)

This murder might have slept in tongueless brass

But for yourself, and the world died an ass.

Now I remember too: here was Piato

Brought forth a knavish sentence once: 'No doubt' — said he —

'But time will make the murderer bring forth himself.'

VINDICE.

Tis well he died, he was a witch.

And now, my lord, since we are in forever:

This work was ours, which else might have been slipped;

And if we wished we could have all here clipped

111

And easily 'scaped. But we hate to bleed
So cowardly: we have enough — i'faith
We're well — our mother turned, our sister true,
We die after a nest of Dukes! Adieu.
(Bow. Exit Vindice and Hippolito followed by Officers.)
ANTONIO.
O how subtly was that murder closed!
Yet now I am Duke.
Now here the law we make our city's god,
And whosoe'er doth dare our rule to flout
T'th'slightst degree, let no man risk doubt
But they shall to the utmost feel the rod.
(Music.)
I will a savior be, bring grace to all:
If in the past you felt the law too strict,
Tomorrow shalt thou feel a sharper whip;
The reign of restless lust is at its fall.
Although it sting your sense of independence,
Tis but a trifling loss to curb all deviance;
As bloody anarchy was fee'd loose tolerance,
Precious days of peace will reward our vigilance.
I'll tear the masks from off all sinful faces,
Cleanse the stench of corruption from our sphere,
New-forge the strange and crooked straight and clear,
Blazing holy beacons into darkened places.
The foul polluting filth of ulcerous sin
Must be purged; with those renegades, begin!
(Vindice and Hippolito appear and are executed — two gunshots.)
Our fair city has seen a heavy season;
Pray God their blood may wash away all treason.
And though some loss of freedom overcloud,
Our city shining pure will make you proud.
Thus be the end all tragedy, and justly.
Bear up those bodies. The scene disgusts me.
*(Officers dispose of bodies, guard with guns. Enter Castiza to Antonio.
He gives her a gold coin. She kneels to him. Pietro and Lord close the
curtain.)*

End of Play

PROPERTY LIST

Masks
Skull
Towels, lotion
Silver coins
Gold coins
Glass of wine
Poison
Daggers
Dress form
Letter
Ring
Bloody bag
Banquet table with food and drink
Swords
Crown

SOUND EFFECTS

Music
Britten's *The Rape of Lucretia*
Music from Verdi's *Otello*
Thunder
Gunshots

NEW PLAYS

★ **THE EXONERATED by Jessica Blank and Erik Jensen.** Six interwoven stories paint a picture of an American criminal justice system gone horribly wrong and six brave souls who persevered to survive it. "The #1 play of the year...intense and deeply affecting..." *–NY Times.* "Riveting. Simple, honest storytelling that demands reflection." *–A.P.* "Artful and moving...pays tribute to the resilience of human hearts and minds." *–Variety.* "Stark...riveting...cunningly orchestrated." *–The New Yorker.* "Hard-hitting, powerful, and socially relevant." *–Hollywood Reporter.* [7M, 3W] ISBN: 0-8222-1946-8

★ **STRING FEVER by Jacquelyn Reingold.** Lily juggles the big issues: turning forty, artificial insemination and the elusive scientific Theory of Everything in this Off-Broadway comedy hit. "Applies the elusive rules of string theory to the conundrums of one woman's love life. Think *Sex and the City* meets *Copenhagen.*" *–NY Times.* "A funny offbeat and touching look at relationships...an appealing romantic comedy populated by oddball characters." *–NY Daily News.* "Where kooky, zany, and madcap meet...whimsically winsome." *–NY Magazine.* "STRING FEVER will have audience members happily stringing along." *–TheaterMania.com.* "Reingold's language is surprising, inventive, and unique." *–nytheatre.com.* "...[a] whimsical comic voice." *–Time Out.* [3M, 3W (doubling)] ISBN: 0-8222-1952-2

★ **DEBBIE DOES DALLAS adapted by Erica Schmidt, composed by Andrew Sherman, conceived by Susan L. Schwartz.** A modern morality tale told as a comic musical of tragic proportions as the classic film is brought to the stage. "A scream! A saucy, tongue-in-cheek romp." *–The New Yorker.* "Hilarious! DEBBIE manages to have it all: beauty, brains and a great sense of humor!" *–Time Out.* "Shamelessly silly, shrewdly self-aware and proud of being naughty. Great fun!" *–NY Times.* "Racy and raucous, a lighthearted, fast-paced thoroughly engaging and hilarious send-up." *–NY Daily News.* [3M, 5W] ISBN: 0-8222-1955-7

★ **THE MYSTERY PLAYS by Roberto Aguirre-Sacasa.** Two interrelated one acts, loosely based on the tradition of the medieval mystery plays. "... stylish, spine-tingling...Mr. Aguirre-Sacasa uses standard tricks of horror stories, borrowing liberally from masters like Kafka, Lovecraft, Hitchcock...But his mastery of the genre is his own...irresistible." *–NY Times.* "Undaunted by the special-effects limitations of theatre, playwright and *Marvel* comic-book writer Roberto Aguirre-Sacasa maps out some creepy twilight zones in THE MYSTERY PLAYS, an engaging, related pair of one acts...The theatre may rarely deliver shocks equivalent to, say, *Dawn of the Dead*, but Aguirre-Sacasa's work is fine compensation." *–Time Out.* [4M, 2W] ISBN: 0-8222-2038-5

★ **THE JOURNALS OF MIHAIL SEBASTIAN by David Auburn.** This epic one-man play spans eight tumultuous years and opens a uniquely personal window on the Romanian Holocaust and the Second World War. "Powerful." *–NY Times.* "[THE JOURNALS OF MIHAIL SEBASTIAN] allows us to glimpse the idiosyncratic effects of that awful history on one intelligent, pragmatic, recognizably real man..." *–NY Newsday.* [3M, 5W] ISBN: 0-8222-2006-7

★ **LIVING OUT by Lisa Loomer.** The story of the complicated relationship between a Salvadoran nanny and the Anglo lawyer she works for. "A stellar new play. Searingly funny." *–The New Yorker.* "Both generous and merciless, equally enjoyable and disturbing." *–NY Newsday.* "A bitingly funny new comedy. The plight of working mothers is explored from two pointedly contrasting perspectives in this sympathetic, sensitive new play." *–Variety.* [2M, 6W] ISBN: 0-8222-1994-8

DRAMATISTS PLAY SERVICE, INC.
440 Park Avenue South, New York, NY 10016 212-683-8960 Fax 212-213-1539
postmaster@dramatists.com www.dramatists.com

NEW PLAYS

★ **MATCH by Stephen Belber.** Mike and Lisa Davis interview a dancer and choreographer about his life, but it is soon evident that their agenda will either ruin or inspire them—and definitely change their lives forever. "Prolific laughs and ear-to-ear smiles." –*NY Magazine.* "Uproariously funny, deeply moving, enthralling theater. Stephen Belber's MATCH has great beauty and tenderness, and abounds in wit." –*NY Daily News.* "Three and a half out of four stars." –*USA Today.* "A theatrical steeplechase that leads straight from outrageous bitchery to unadorned, heartfelt emotion." –*Wall Street Journal.* [2M, 1W] ISBN: 0-8222-2020-2

★ **HANK WILLIAMS: LOST HIGHWAY by Randal Myler and Mark Harelik.** The story of the beloved and volatile country-music legend Hank Williams, featuring twenty-five of his most unforgettable songs. "[LOST HIGHWAY has] the exhilarating feeling of Williams on stage in a particular place on a particular night…serves up classic country with the edges raw and the energy hot…By the end of the play, you've traveled on a profound emotional journey: LOST HIGHWAY transports its audience and communicates the inspiring message of the beauty and richness of Williams' songs…forceful, clear-eyed, moving, impressive." –*Rolling Stone.* "…honors a very particular musical talent with care and energy… smart, sweet, poignant." –*NY Times.* [7M, 3W] ISBN: 0-8222-1985-9

★ **THE STORY by Tracey Scott Wilson.** An ambitious black newspaper reporter goes against her editor to investigate a murder and finds the *best* story…but at what cost? "A singular new voice…deeply emotional, deeply intellectual, and deeply musical…" –*The New Yorker.* "…a conscientious and absorbing new drama…" –*NY Times.* "…a riveting, tough-minded drama about race, reporting and the truth…" –*A.P.* "… a stylish, attention-holding script that ends on a chilling note that will leave viewers with much to talk about." –*Curtain Up.* [2M, 7W (doubling, flexible casting)] ISBN: 0-8222-1998-0

★ **OUR LADY OF 121st STREET by Stephen Adly Guirgis.** The body of Sister Rose, beloved Harlem nun, has been stolen, reuniting a group of life-challenged childhood friends who square off as they wait for her return. "A scorching and dark new comedy… Mr. Guirgis has one of the finest imaginations for dialogue to come along in years." –*NY Times.* "Stephen Guirgis may be the best playwright in America under forty." –*NY Magazine.* [8M, 4W] ISBN: 0-8222-1965-4

★ **HOLLYWOOD ARMS by Carrie Hamilton and Carol Burnett.** The coming-of-age story of a dreamer who manages to escape her bleak life and follow her romantic ambitions to stardom. Based on Carol Burnett's bestselling autobiography, *One More Time.* "…pure theatre and pure entertainment…" –*Talkin' Broadway.* "…a warm, fuzzy evening of theatre." –*BrodwayBeat.com.* "…chuckles and smiles of recognition or surprise flow naturally…a remarkable slice of life." –*TheatreScene.net.* [5M, 5W, 1 girl] ISBN: 0-8222-1959-X

★ **INVENTING VAN GOGH by Steven Dietz.** A haunting and hallucinatory drama about the making of art, the obsession to create and the fine line that separates truth from myth. "Like a van Gogh painting, Dietz's story is a gorgeous example of excess—one that remakes reality with broad, well-chosen brush strokes. At evening's end, we're left with the author's resounding opinions on art and artifice, and provoked by his constant query into which is greater: van Gogh's art or his violent myth." –*Phoenix New Times.* "Dietz's writing is never simple. It is always brilliant. Shaded, compressed, direct, lucid—he frames his subject with a remarkable understanding of painting as a physical experience." –*Tucson Citizen.* [4M, 1W] ISBN: 0-8222-1954-9

DRAMATISTS PLAY SERVICE, INC.
440 Park Avenue South, New York, NY 10016 212-683-8960 Fax 212-213-1539
postmaster@dramatists.com www.dramatists.com

NEW PLAYS

★ **INTIMATE APPAREL by Lynn Nottage.** The moving and lyrical story of a turn-of-the-century black seamstress whose gifted hands and sewing machine are the tools she uses to fashion her dreams from the whole cloth of her life's experiences. "…Nottage's play has a delicacy and eloquence that seem absolutely right for the time she is depicting…" –*NY Daily News.* "…thoughtful, affecting…The play offers poignant commentary on an era when the cut and color of one's dress—and of course, skin—determined whom one could and could not marry, sleep with, even talk to in public." –*Variety.* [2M, 4W] ISBN: 0-8222-2009-1

★ **BROOKLYN BOY by Donald Margulies.** A witty and insightful look at what happens to a writer when his novel hits the bestseller list. "The characters are beautifully drawn, the dialogue sparkles…" –*nytheatre.com.* "Few playwrights have the mastery to smartly investigate so much through a laugh-out-loud comedy that combines the vintage subject matter of successful writer-returning-to-ethnic-roots with the familiar mid-life crisis." –*Show Business Weekly.* [4M, 3W] ISBN: 0-8222-2074-1

★ **CROWNS by Regina Taylor.** Hats become a springboard for an exploration of black history and identity in this celebratory musical play. "Taylor pulls off a Hat Trick: She scores thrice, turning CROWNS into an artful amalgamation of oral history, fashion show, and musical theater…" –*TheatreMania.com.* "…wholly theatrical…Ms. Taylor has created a show that seems to arise out of spontaneous combustion, as if a bevy of department-store customers simultaneously decided to stage a revival meeting in the changing room." –*NY Times.* [1M, 6W (2 musicians)] ISBN: 0-8222-1963-8

★ **EXITS AND ENTRANCES by Athol Fugard.** The story of a relationship between a young playwright on the threshold of his career and an aging actor who has reached the end of his. "[Fugard] can say more with a single line than most playwrights convey in an entire script…Paraphrasing the title, it's safe to say this drama, making its memorable entrance into our consciousness, is unlikely to exit as long as a theater exists for exceptional work." –*Variety.* "A thought-provoking, elegant and engrossing new play…" –*Hollywood Reporter.* [2M] ISBN: 0-8222-2041-5

★ **BUG by Tracy Letts.** A thriller featuring a pair of star-crossed lovers in an Oklahoma City motel facing a bug invasion, paranoia, conspiracy theories and twisted psychological motives. "…obscenely exciting…top-flight craftsmanship. Buckle up and brace yourself…" –*NY Times.* "…[a] thoroughly outrageous and thoroughly entertaining play…the possibility of enemies, real and imagined, to squash has never been more theatrical." –*A.P.* [3M, 2W] ISBN: 0-8222-2016-4

★ **THOM PAIN (BASED ON NOTHING) by Will Eno.** An ordinary man muses on childhood, yearning, disappointment and loss, as he draws the audience into his last-ditch plea for empathy and enlightenment. "It's one of those treasured nights in the theater—treasured nights anywhere, for that matter—that can leave you both breathless with exhilaration and…in a puddle of tears." –*NY Times.* "Eno's words…are familiar, but proffered in a way that is constantly contradictory to our expectations. Beckett is certainly among his literary ancestors." –*nytheatre.com.* [1M] ISBN: 0-8222-2076-8

★ **THE LONG CHRISTMAS RIDE HOME by Paula Vogel.** Past, present and future collide on a snowy Christmas Eve for a troubled family of five. "…[a] lovely and hauntingly original family drama…a work that breathes so much life into the theater." –*Time Out.* "…[a] delicate visual feast…" –*NY Times.* "…brutal and lovely…the overall effect is magical." –*NY Newsday.* [3M, 3W] ISBN: 0-8222-2003-2

DRAMATISTS PLAY SERVICE, INC.
440 Park Avenue South, New York, NY 10016 212-683-8960 Fax 212-213-1539
postmaster@dramatists.com www.dramatists.com